FOOTBALL ENGLISH
ELEMENTARY

Mark Bailey and Andrew Talbot

SUPPORTED BY:

Copyright ©2022 HATRIQA Limited

All rights reserved. Apart from any use permitted under UK copyright law, no part of this publication may be reproduced, stored in a retrieval system, or transmitted in any form or by any means, electronic or mechanical, including photocopying, recording, or otherwise without prior written permission from the Publisher or under license permitting restricted copying in the United Kingdom from the Copyright Licensing Agency Limited. Further details of such licenses (for reprographic reproduction) may be obtained from the Copyright Licensing Agency Limited, www.cla.co.uk.

ISBN 9781739095291

First Edition January 2021
Second Edition January 2023
Third Edition April 2025

Published by HATRIQA Limited
Lower Ground Floor
7 Coleherne Road
London SW10 9BS

EDITOR Nicole Elliott
PUBLISHER Tim Gentles
ILLUSTRATIONS Marcus Marritt
DESIGN Lucy Allen
TYPESETTING Jennifer Ferguson/Dulcius Design

Special thanks to Hank Steinbrecher, Joan Laporta, Emma Jones MBE, The Enterprise Nation Bus, Felipe Anderson, Dan Freedman, Alison Edgar MBE, Issei Yokoi, Andy Downer, UCL Institute of Education, UCL EDUCATE, UCL Innovation and Enterprise

Orders are available through our website at www.hatriqa.com or by emailing orders@hatriqa.com.

A catalogue record for this title is available from the British Library.

Printed and bound by CPI Group (UK) Ltd, Croydon, CR0 4YY

Introduction

The content in this book is based on first-hand experience of teaching elite professional players; interviews with Premier League players, clubs and Football English teachers; and personal experience of playing for a football team in a foreign country.

Football English Elementary provides essential vocabulary players and coaches need to communicate before, during and after a game – both on and off the field. It also includes fundamental language required for daily life, while grammar points are structured to correspond to CEFR guidelines.

How to use this book

The book is designed as a stand-alone tool and also supports teachers working with students using HATRIQA's self-study Workbook and the HATRIQA mobile app. Each unit is designed like a lesson, so the content builds step-by-step, and each unit builds on the previous one. For this reason, it is recommended that teachers simply follow the content in order. Audio transcripts and answer keys can be found in the back of the book.

 0.1 To access all the audio files, visit www.hatriqa.com/audio/fe1
No password or login is needed.

Listen to the recording

HATRIQA Workbook & App

For the optimum learning experience, we recommend using this book in tandem with the HATRIQA Workbook and HATRIQA mobile app, available at www.hatriqa.com. Both the Workbook and app deliver ready-to-go self-study lessons to reinforce learning. The core content of this Textbook is mirrored in the Workbook and app, so they can be used as complementary tools. For example, the Workbook and app content could be given as a lesson-review or pre-lesson task.

About the authors

MARK BAILEY: Mark is the co-founder of HATRIQA and a Teaching Fellow at University College London (UCL), Institute of Education. He has written a dissertation at UCL on the provision of Football English in the English Premier League and has taught numerous professional players and management. He has nearly 20 years' experience teaching English in the UK, Japan and South America.

ANDREW TALBOT: Born in Norway and raised in England, Andrew has travelled extensively and lived in Japan, Russia and Argentina. He is a published author of fiction and non-fiction, and has nearly two decades of international ESL experience. He lives in Brazil with his family.

Contents

	Core Football Vocabulary	6
	English Spelling and Pronunciation	10
	Meet the Teams	15
UNIT 1	**Player Positions and Personal Information** Present simple *be*	18
UNIT 2	**Football Actions** Present simple (+/−)	24
UNIT 3	**Rules of the Game** Present simple (?)	29
UNIT 4	**Football Kit** Possessives, singular and plural	36
UNIT 5	**Daily Routine** Present simple for routines	42
	Review UNITS 1–5	48
UNIT 6	**The Body** *Can*	49
UNIT 7	**Describing Players** *Be* + adjective / football expressions	55
UNIT 8	**Playing in a Game** Imperatives	61
UNIT 9	**After the Game** Past simple	67
UNIT 10	**Fixtures and Results** Future tense	75
	Review UNITS 6–10	82
	Grammar Reference	83
	Irregular Verbs	95
	Listening Scripts	96
	Answer Key	100

Core Football Vocabulary

Core Football Vocabulary

Core Football Vocabulary

Core Football Vocabulary

English Spelling and Pronunciation

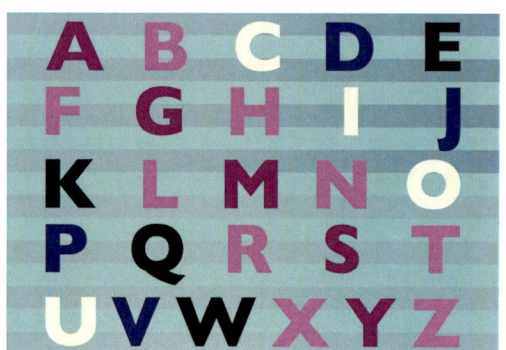

This is the English alphabet. Can you say all the sounds?

The English alphabet has 26 letters, but there are 44 different sounds in the English language!

Part 1: Spelling

Listen to the recording

0.1 🔊 **Exercise 1**

Listen and (circle) the letter you hear.

1. E / I
2. Y / I
3. M / N
4. R / H
5. B / P
6. K / Q
7. U / W
8. E / A
9. B / V
10. S / Z

> **Useful expressions**
> "How do you spell that?"
> "Sorry, could you say that again?"

Listen to the recording

0.2 🔊 **Exercise 2**

Listen to the spellings and write down the famous football cities.

1. _____
2. _____
3. _____
4. _____
5. _____ City

> **Did you know?**
> The club with the most letters in the world is Scottish team *Inverness Caledonian Thistle FC*!

Exercise 3

Practise spelling these words with a partner. Can you spell the words correctly? Can your partner write down the words correctly?

Person A: Spell one of your words. Your partner will write it down. Then listen to the word your partner spells and try to write that down. Take turns.

Person B: Listen to the word your partner spells and try to write it down. Then spell one of your words. Your partner will write that down. Take turns.

> **Did you know?**
> We use the words *capital* and *small* to describe letters. For example:
> **A** = "capital a"
> **a** = "small a"

Person A					
Your words	football	win	defender	post	London
Your partner's words					

					Person B
United	pitch	forward	lose	soccer	Your words
					Your partner's words

English Spelling and Pronunciation

Part 2: English Sounds

Listen to the recording

0.3 🔊 **Exercise 1**

Look at the chart. Listen and repeat the **short vowel** sounds and the example words.

> **Did you know?**
> The /ə/ sound is called a *schwa*. The schwa is the most common sound in English!

Symbol		Usual spelling		But also!
e	penalty /ˈpenəlti/	e → ten, seven, twenty, Mexico		friend, breakfast, header
ɪ	kick /kɪk/	i → Italy, six, is, it, win		English, United, gym
æ	flag /flæg/	a → bad, hand, tackle, man		
ʌ	London /ˈlʌndən/	u → umbrella, bus, number, hurry		son, brother, double
ʊ	football /ˈfʊtbɔːl/	u → full, sugar oo → good, book, look		could, woman
ɒ	soccer /ˈsɒkə(r)/	o → shot, coffee, from, holiday		what, want, watch
ə	centre /ˈsentə(r)/	*Many different spellings, always unstressed* defender, about, police, famous		

Listen to the recording

0.4 🔊 **Exercise 2**

Look at the chart. Listen and repeat the **long vowel** sounds and the example words.

Symbol		Usual spelling		But also!
iː	team /tiːm/	ee → feet, meet ea → please, eat	e → she, we	people, key
ɜː	shirt /ʃɜːt/	er → person, verb ur → nurse, hurt	ir → bird, third	work, world, word
ɔː	ball /bɔːl/	or → short, corner al → tall, call	aw → awful	water, four, bought
uː	boot /buːt/	oo → shoot, food ue → blue, continue	u_e → rule, tube ew → few, new	two, you, juice
ɑː	pass /pɑːs/	ar → car, park a → father, fast		heart

0.5 🔊 Exercise 3

A diphthong is a sound with two vowels in one syllable. Look at the chart. Listen and repeat the **diphthong vowel** sounds and the example words.

Listen to the recording

Symbol		Usual spelling	But also!
ɪə	year /jɪə(r)/	ear → near, hear eer → beer, cheer ere → here, we're	idea
eə	penalty area /ˈpenəlti ˌeəriə/	air → chair, hair are → careful, share	there, their, where
eɪ	player /ˈpleɪə(r)/	a_e → name, late ai → training, rain ay → say, pay	eight, they, great
ɔɪ	ball boy /ˈbɔːl bɔɪ/	oi → toilet, noise oy → toy, enjoy	
aɪ	United /juˈnaɪtɪd/	i_e → bike, nice y → my, by igh → right, light	buy
əʊ	goal /ɡəʊl/	o → hello, open o_e → phone, wrote oa → coat, boat	window
aʊ	foul /faʊl/	ow → crowd, town ou → house, out	
ʊə	Europe /ˈjʊərəp/	*A very unusual sound* Euro, sure, tour	

English Spelling and Pronunciation

Listen to the recording

0.6 🔊 **Exercise 4**

Look at the chart. Listen and repeat the **consonant** sounds and the example words.

p	b	t	d	tʃ	dʒ
post, penalty, jump	ball, bench, hobby	tackle, table, kicked	draw, played, dog	pitch, chip, China	manager, danger, jump
k	**g**	**f**	**v**	**θ**	**ð**
corner, catch, kick	goalkeeper, league, go	first, phone, laugh	volley, video, of	throw-in, healthy, teeth	mother, the, this
s	**z**	**ʃ**	**ʒ**	**m**	**n**
score, city, police	lazy, gloves, has	shoot, special, nation	First Division, leisure, visual	midfielder, match, thumb	net, funny, know
ŋ	**j**	**l**	**r**	**w**	**h**
winger, passing, English	yellow card, onion, view	lose, feel, smelly	red card, right, wrong	win, one, where	header, hungry, who

Key:

voiced   unvoiced

Listen to the recording

0.7 🔊 **Exercise 5**

Listen and (circle) the words you hear.

1. shoot   shirt   4. play   pay
2. ball   tall   5. score   more
3. goal   girl   6. header   defender

Meet the Teams

Welcome to *Football English*!

In this book, you'll learn how to talk about your life – and a lot about football!
Every unit will talk about Locomotive London, a football club from England.
Meet the men's and women's teams!

Part 1: Locomotive London Men's Team

Exercise 1

Match the information about the Locomotive London men's team (**1–7**) to the pictures (**A–G**).

1. Locomotive London stadium ___
2. Club badge ___
3. Head Coach, Joe ___
4. Star player, Harry Jones ___
5. Home shirt ___
6. Number of league titles ___
7. Goalkeeper, Luke Peterson ___

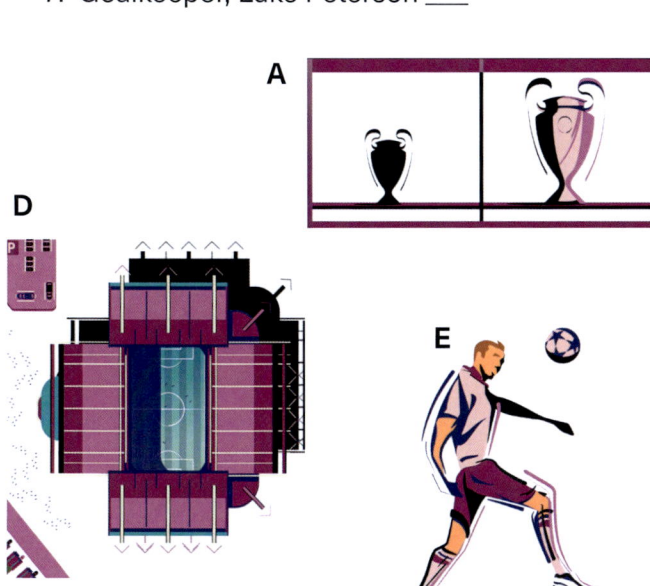
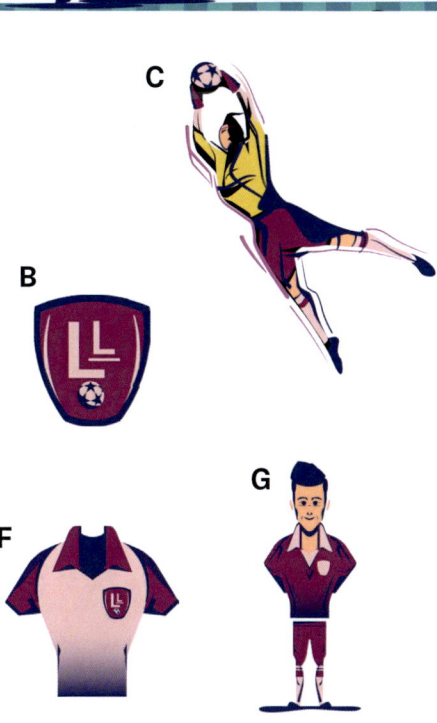

Exercise 2

Complete the information about the men's team using the words from the box.

> players   55,000   Locomotive   43   Stadium   England   2017

Club name	_____ London
Year founded	_____
Location	London, _____
_____ name	Champion Ground
Stadium capacity	_____
Head Coach / age	Joe Cardoso / _____
Famous _____	Luca Liberato, Taka Sato, Harry Jones

Part 2: Locomotive London Women's Team

Exercise 1

Complete the information about the Locomotive London women's team using the words from the box.

> ~~stadium~~   Coach   newer   captain   won

Locomotive London's women play in the same [1.] *stadium* as the men's team – Champion Ground. But the women's team is [2.] _____ than the men's team. It was only founded in 2020, but they've already [3.] _____ two trophies – one English Women's League and one England Women's Cup.

Their Head [4.] _____, Jemma Haynes, is one of the best coaches in the world. She won an Olympic medal and many trophies in Europe and the USA. Their star player and [5.] _____, Lucy Harper, played in the USA before she moved to London. Many people think she'll win the Women's Ballon d'Or soon!

Meet the Teams

Exercise 2

Look at the video game profiles of three players from the women's team. Match the players and positions (**1–3**) to the descriptions (**a–c**).

1. Kim is a defender.
2. Haruka is a midfielder.
3. Yuna is a forward.

a. She's good at passing.
b. She's fast and good at shooting.
c. She's strong.

> **Video games**
>
> Some video games use abbreviations – short words – to describe players.
>
> **PAC** = pace (speed)   **DRI** = dribbling
> **SHO** = shooting   **DEF** = defending
> **PAS** = passing   **PHY** = physical (height, strength)

Now you're ready to learn English and talk about football! Let's kick off!

UNIT 1

Lesson Goals

Vocabulary: Player positions
Grammar: Present simple *be*
Skills: Talking about personal information

Player Positions and Personal Information

Miguel is a new player at Locomotive London.

When players join a new team, it's important to make friends.

What questions do you ask new players?

Miguel

Part 1: Vocabulary

Exercise 1

A new player needs to be able to talk about their **position** – where they play.

a. What's your **position**? Look at the picture and tell your partner where you play.

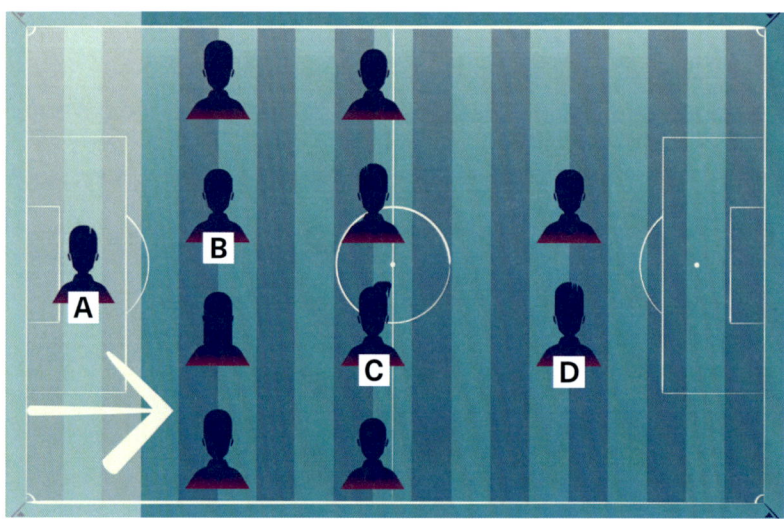

b. Can you match the players (**A–D**) above to their positions (**1–4**) below?

1. Defender   2. Goalkeeper   3. Forward   4. Midfielder

UNIT 1 | Player Positions and Personal Information

c. Complete the positions below with the words from the box.

full   centre   midfielder   centre   winger   coach

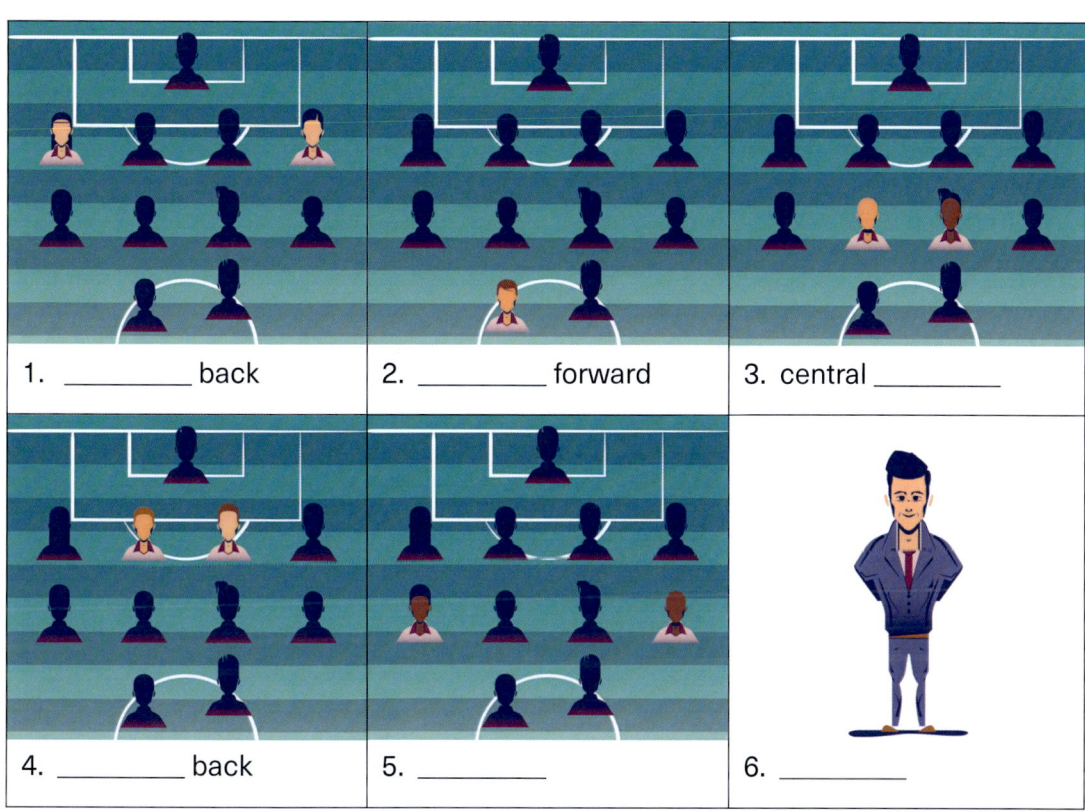

1. _____ back
2. _____ forward
3. central _____
4. _____ back
5. _____
6. _____

Exercise 2

Complete the sentences.

1. Haaland and Mbappé are f___ ___w___ ___ds.
2. You're a w___ ___g___ ___.
3. Pep Guardiola is a co___ ___ ___.
4. Ona Batlle & Selma Bacha are f___ ___l b___ ___ks.
5. Bellingham is a ce___ ___r___l m___df___ ___l___ ___r.
6. I'm a _____.

> **Number 9?**
> There are many other names for a **centre forward**. They are sometimes called a *number 9*, an *attacker* or a *striker*.

19

UNIT 1 | Player Positions and Personal Information

Part 2: Grammar

This lesson uses the verb **be** (am/is/are).

+	I **am** a forward. You/We/They **are**...	Bellingham **is** a midfielder. He/She/It **is**...
?	**Am** I a forward? **Are** you/we/they...?	**Is** he/she a coach?
−	I **am not** a coach. You/We/They **are not**...	He/She **is not** a forward.

We can also use contractions in positive and negative sentences.

+	I**'m** a forward. You/We/They**'re**...	He/She/It**'s**...
−	I**'m not** a coach. You/We/They **aren't**...	He/She **isn't** a forward.

Did you know?
We say **are** for football teams.
Example: Liverpool **are** my favourite team.
Not: ~~Liverpool **is** my favourite team.~~

See p83 for more about present simple **be**.

Exercise 1

Football quiz

The verb **be** is used a lot to give **personal information**. How much do you know about these famous players?

a. Complete the questions and answers.

Example: **Q:** ____*Is*____ Haaland a defender?

A: No, he ___*isn't*___ . He ___*'s*___ ___*a*___ forward.

1. **Q:** _____ Mara Alber a goalkeeper?
   A: No, she _____. She _____ _____ winger.
2. **Q:** _____ Williams and Yamal full backs?
   A: No, they _____. They _____.
3. **Q:** How old _____ Jude Bellingham?
   A: He _____ _____ years old.
4. **Q:** Where _____ Maradona and Messi from?
   A: They _____ from _____.

b. Now ask your partner the questions. Do they know the answers?

UNIT 1 | Player Positions and Personal Information

Part 3: Listening

1.1 🔊 Exercise 1

Locomotive London players Jack and Harry are talking at the training ground.

Listen to the recording

a. Listen to the conversation. Who are they talking about? Circle the correct answer.

| a new player | another team | the coach |

b. Listen again and choose the correct words to complete the sentences.

1. Where's Miguel from? He's from *Italy / Spain / Mexico*.
2. What position is Miguel? He's a *defender / midfielder / forward*.
3. What position is Harry? He's a *defender / midfielder / forward*.

Part 4: Practice

When we meet new people, we often ask "Where are you from?" In the conversation in Part 3, we heard that Miguel is from **Spain**. He's **Spanish**.

Exercise 1

How well do you know country names in English?

Match the country names below (**1–6**) to the football shirts on the next page (**A–F**).

1. Brazil ___
2. Spain ___
3. France ___
4. England ___
5. Japan ___
6. Germany ___

UNIT 1 | Player Positions and Personal Information

Manager or coach?

Managers choose who plays and where they play. At professional clubs they also choose which players to buy and sell. **Coaches** are like teachers, helping players on the training ground to become better and better. At professional clubs, a manager is also sometimes called a *Head Coach*.

Does your team have a **Manager**, a **Coach** or both?

Exercise 2

Rearrange the letters to make **nationalities**. Then match them to the country names.

(ngelish)	_____	Brazil
(nchefr)	_____	England
(zlaiibran)	*Brazilian*	Spain
(jpanesea)	_____	Japan
(gmrnea)	_____	France
(spnisha)	_____	Germany

Where is football from?

The UK? The USA? Brazil? No! Football is from China. It was first played in 476 BC!

Exercise 3

Yes/no questions

Test your partner's football knowledge. Ask them 4 *yes/no* questions about famous players' countries or nationalities.

Examples:

A: Is Jude Bellingham from Japan?
B: No, he isn't. He's from England.
A: Are Ona Batlle and Vicky Lopez Spanish?
B: Yes, they are.

UNIT 1 | Player Positions and Personal Information

Part 5: Speaking and Writing

Exercise 1

Media interview
You're a new player at a club and a football magazine wants to write about you.

a. First, complete the journalist's questions below with the words from the box. Then, write your answers to the questions.

> who   what   how   what   are   is   am   are   your   you   is

1. What _____ _____ name? My _____ .
2. _____ old _____ you? I _____ _____ years old.
3. Where _____ _____ from? I _____ .
4. _____ is your position? I _____ .
5. _____ _____ your favourite player? _____ .
6. _____ is your favourite thing about football? _____ !

b. Now, practise the conversation with your partner!

UNIT 2

Football Actions

Lesson Goals

Vocabulary: Football actions
Grammar: Present simple (+/–)
Skills: Describing players' actions

In Unit 1, you learned about **player positions**. Now, you'll learn what **actions** these positions do.

Part 1: Vocabulary

Exercise 1

a. What's your **position**? Which of the **actions** below do you do?

b. Can you match the pictures (**A–H**) to the actions (**1–8**)?

1. Pass ___
2. Tackle ___
3. Cross ___
4. Clear ___
5. Shoot ___
6. Save ___
7. Head ___
8. Mark ___

UNIT 2 | Football Actions

Exercise 2

Choose the correct words to complete the sentences.

1. I'm a forward, so I always *shoot / save / mark*.
2. Donnarumma is a goalkeeper, so he *crosses / saves / heads* the ball to stop a goal.
3. Naomi Girma and Emily Fox are centre backs, so they *shoot / save / head* the ball a lot.
4. Jack is a central midfielder, so he *passes / shoots / saves* the ball a lot.
5. Linda Caicedo is a winger, so she *crosses / saves / marks* the ball a lot.
6. Defenders and midfielders *tackle / shoot / cross* the other team's players.

Part 2: Grammar

This lesson uses the **present simple**. We use the present simple to talk about:

- Something that's **true now** – I **live** in London.
- Something that **happens regularly** – I **play** football on Saturdays.
- Something that's **always true** – Manchester United **play** at Old Trafford.

+	I **pass** the ball. You **pass** the ball. We **pass** the ball. They **pass** the ball.	Jack **plays** for Locomotive. He **passes** the ball. She **fouls** the forward. It **looks** offside.
?	Do I/you/we/they **pass** the ball?	**Does** he/she **pass** the ball?
–	I/you/we/they **don't** pass the ball.	He/she **doesn't** pass the ball.

See p84 for more about the present simple.

Did you know?
If you score 3 goals in a game, it is called a **hat-trick**.

Exercise 1

Complete the sentences on the next page using only two of the words in brackets.

Example:

____He____ ____tackles____ the forward to stop a goal.

(tackle) (he) (tackles) (it)

UNIT 2 | Football Actions

1. _____ _____ the ball when it's in the air.
   (tackle) (I) (head) (heads) (tackles)
2. _____ _____ the forward by kicking her.
   (she) (shoots) (fouls) (foul) (play)
3. Harry and Jack are midfielders.
   _____ _____ the ball very well.
   (he) (they) (go) (pass) (passing)
4. Good forwards score a lot of goals because _____ _____ a lot.
   (he) (they) (pass) (shoot) (clear)

> **Nutmeg**
> A *nutmeg* happens when a player kicks the ball through their opponent's legs. It's sometimes called a *panna*.

Part 3: Listening

2.1 🔊 Exercise 1

Two players for Locomotive London – Jack and Harry – are playing a football quiz on their smartphones.

Listen to the recording

a. Look at the player names in the box. Do you know what actions they do a lot?

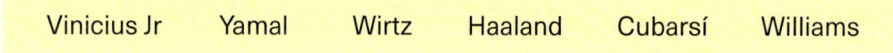

Vinicius Jr   Yamal   Wirtz   Haaland   Cubarsí   Williams

b. Listen to the conversation and (circle) the names you hear in the box.

c. Write the names you heard into the table below. Now, listen again and complete the table with ✓ or ✗.

Name	Tackles	Heads	Passes	Crosses	Scores
Wirtz					

Part 4: Practice

> In the conversation in Part 3, we heard that:
> Florian Wirtz passes the ball. (+)
> Lamine Yamal **doesn't** tackle. (−)
>
> I/you/we/they = do ⟶ I **don't** tackle.
> He/she/it = does ⟶ He **doesn't** tackle.

Exercise 1

Complete the sentences using **don't/doesn't**.

Example:
Defenders ___don't___ shoot a lot.

1. Goalkeepers _____ cross the ball.
2. Forwards _____ save the ball.
3. Spain _____ play in pink shirts.
4. Musiala _____ play in defence.
5. I _____ .

UNIT 2 | Football Actions

Part 5: Speaking and Writing

Exercise 1

A football website wants to ask about you and your team.

a. First, complete the questions below. Then, write your answers to the questions.

1. Wh_____'s your name? My _____ _____ _____.
2. _____ old are you? I _____ _____ years old.
3. Wh_____ are you from? I _____ _____ _____.
4. _____ your position? I'm _____ _____.
5. On your team, who sh_____ the most? _____ _____ the most!
6. On your team, who t_____ the most? _____ _____ the most!
7. On your team, who p_____ the most? _____ _____ the most!
8. On your team, who sa_____ the most? _____!

b. Now, practise the conversation with your partner!

> **Football or soccer?**
> People in the UK and Ireland say *football*, but people in the USA, Canada, Australia and South Africa say *soccer*.

UNIT 3

Lesson Goals
Vocabulary: Rules of the game
Grammar: Present simple (?)
Skills: Describing events in a game

Rules of the Game

The rules of the game are very important.

Which rules do you know in English?

In this lesson, you'll learn how to talk about them in English. Let's kick off!

Part 1: Vocabulary

Exercise 1

Match the pictures (**A–F**) to the actions (**1–6**).

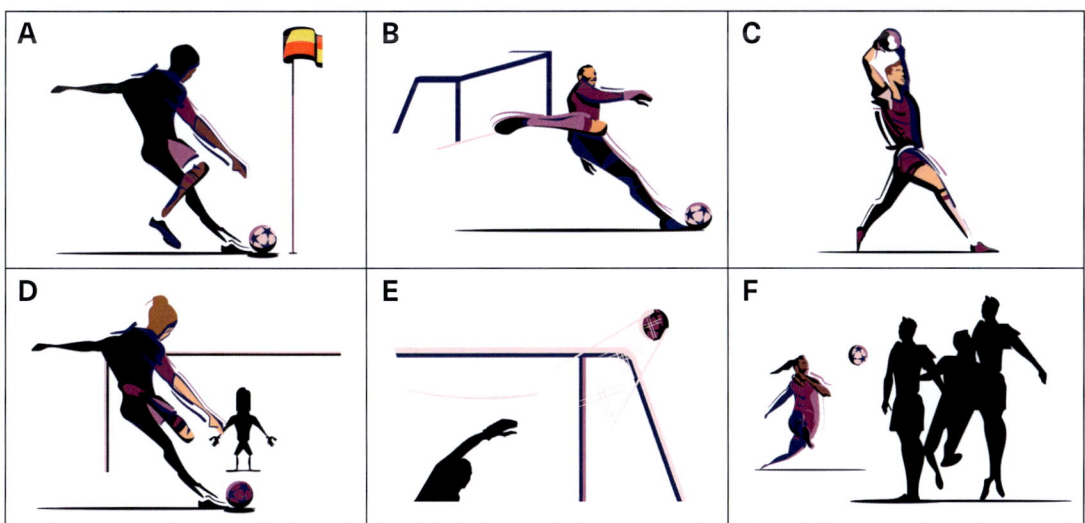

1. throw-in ___
2. goal kick ___
3. free kick ___
4. corner ___
5. penalty ___
6. goal ___

UNIT 3 | Rules of the Game

Exercise 2

Where do the actions happen on the football pitch? Match the words (**1–6**) to the parts of the pitch (**A–F**).

1. centre circle ___
2. corner flag ___
3. touchline ___
4. the box ___
5. the halfway line ___
6. the goal ___

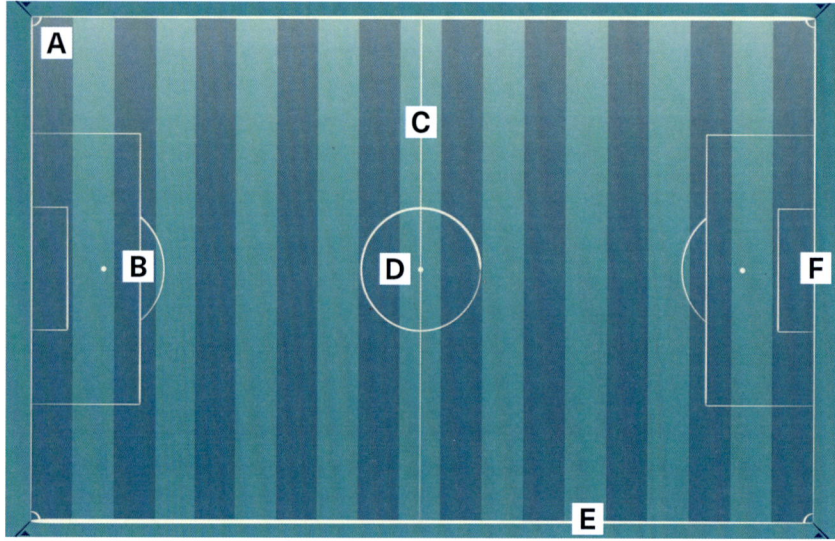

Exercise 3

a. Choose the correct words to complete the sentences.

1. A defender takes a **throw-in** *on the touchline / in the box / in the centre circle*.
2. A forward takes a **penalty** *on the halfway line / in the centre circle / in the box*.
3. **Kick-off** happens *on the touchline / in the box / in the centre circle*.
4. Players take **corners** from *the box / the halfway line / the corner flag*.

b. The above actions are called **set pieces**. Do you know any famous **set-piece takers**?

Example:
Saka takes **free kicks** for England.

> **Did you know?**
> At the start of the game and after half-time, we **kick off** in the centre circle. The fastest ever goal was scored from the **kick-off** by Nawaf Al Abed in Saudi Arabia in 2.4 seconds.

UNIT 3 | Rules of the Game

Part 2: Listening

3.1 🔊 Exercise 1

Harry and Jack are talking to Head Coach, Joe Caldoso. Harry and Jack are the **set-piece takers** for their next game.

Listen to the recording

a. Listen to the conversation. Which 3 **set pieces** do they talk about? (Circle) the correct answers.

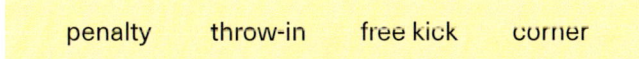

penalty   throw-in   free kick   corner

b. Listen again and write **H** for Harry or **J** for Jack in the correct boxes below.

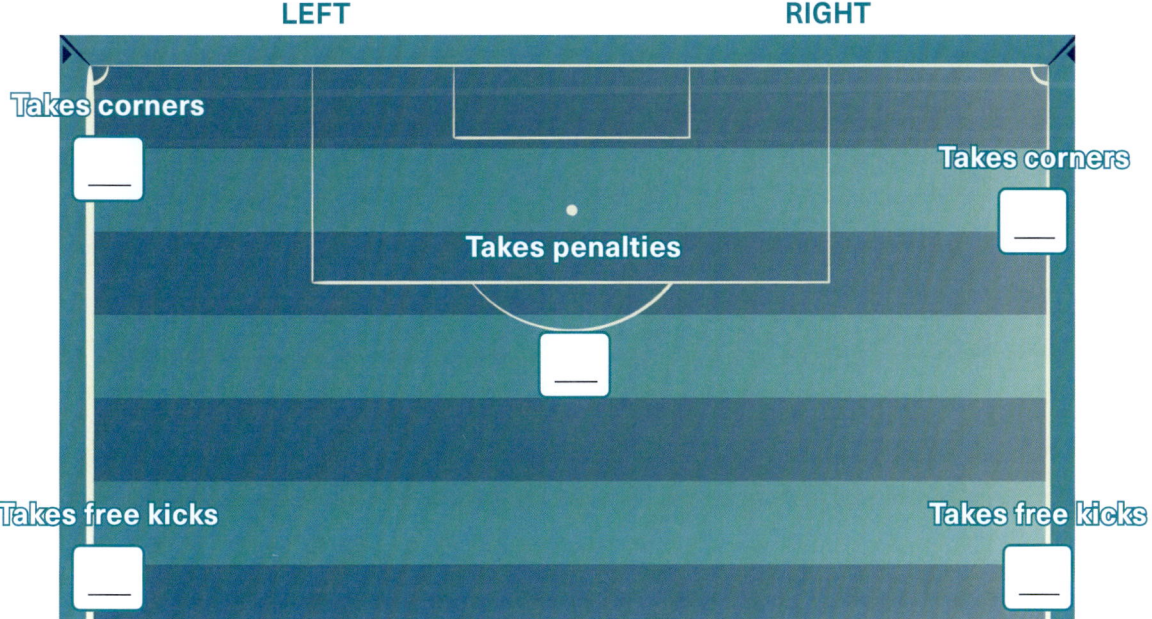

c. Do you think Locomotive London will win their next game? Why or why not?

UNIT 3 | Rules of the Game

3.2 🔊 Exercise 2

Be the ref!
Listen to these actions from a game and (circle) the correct **set piece**.

Listen to the recording

Example:
"It is a foul in the box." = *penalty*

1. penalty / corner / free kick
2. throw-in / goal kick / kick-off
3. corner / penalty / throw-in

Come on, ref!
We often call the referee **ref** for short.

Part 3: Grammar

> This lesson uses the verb **take**. We use it to talk about **set pieces**.
>
> +   Jack **takes** free kicks.
>
> ?   Who **takes** penalties?
>
> −   Harry **doesn't take** corners.

See p85 for more about the present simple.

Exercise 1

Complete the sentences.

Example:
Harry __takes__ penalties.

1. Jack _____ _____ penalties.
2. Harry and Jack _____ free kicks.
3. Who _____ free kicks from the left?
4. Goalkeepers _____ _____ corners.
5. _____ you take throw-ins?
6. I _____ .

Did you know?
In the Premier League, only 3.2% of corners lead to a goal.

UNIT 3 | Rules of the Game

Part 4: Practice

Set pieces happen because of **the rules of the game**. To talk about **the rules of the game**, we use the verb *be*.

Examples:

It**'s** a corner. There **are** two halves of 45 minutes.

Exercise 1

Rearrange these words to make sentences. Then match the sentences (**1–5**) to the pictures (**A–E**).

1. 's / a / throw-in / it _____ ___
2. 's / a / it / free kick _____ ___
3. 's / it / a / foul _____ ___
4. offside / it / 's _____ ___
5. handball / it / 's _____ ___

A B C D E

Exercise 2

Be the commentator!

Look at the scenes from a game (**A–C**) on the next page and describe what you see.

Example (Scene A):

"It's a foul. Then the midfielder takes a free kick, but the goalkeeper saves it."

UNIT 3 | Rules of the Game

Part 5: Speaking and Writing

Exercise 1

Choose the correct words to complete the questions. Then answer the questions about you and your team.

1. Who *take / takes* free kicks in your team?
2. *Do / Does* you shoot with your right foot?
3. *Do / Does* your coach tell you to get in the box?
4. When *do / does* you go near the halfway line?
5. Who's the best player on your team? Where *do / does* he or she play?

Part 6: Extra Time

Exercise 1

Below is the commentary to Harry and Jack's game. Complete the commentary with the words from the box.

> spot   box   touchline   take   scores

"Harry dribbles down the 1._____ and passes to Jack. Jack goes into the 2._____ ... oh, foul... it's a penalty! Who'll 3._____ the penalty? Harry! He puts the ball on the penalty 4._____ ... and... goal! Harry 5._____ and Locomotive London win the game in the final minute! Amazing!"

Exercise 2

Write a commentary about your last game and then tell a partner!

_____
_____
_____
_____
_____
_____
_____
_____
_____
_____
_____
_____
_____
_____

Lesson Goals

Vocabulary: Football kit
Grammar: Possessives, singular and plural
Skills: Describing football kit

UNIT 4
Football Kit

This unit will help you talk about your **football kit** – the clothes you wear to play football. Some teams are given **nicknames** just because of their kit.
For example, *Los Blancos* (the whites) = Real Madrid.
Do you know these other famous teams?
  The Reds = L ___v ___ ___ p ___ ___ l
  The Blues = C h ___ l s ___ ___
  Los Blaugranas (the blue and reds) = B ___ r c ___ l ___ ___ a
Which team has the best kit? What colour is your kit?

Part 1: Vocabulary

Exercise 1

a. Tick (✓) the **kit** you can see:

☐ Boots
☐ Shirt
☐ Shorts
☐ Socks
☐ Shin pads
☐ Gloves

UNIT 4 | Football Kit

b. Complete the sentences (**1–6**) and then match them with the pictures (**A–F**).

1. Their **shorts** are b l ___ ___. ___
2. His **socks** are b l ___ ___ k. ___
3. His **shirt** is w h ___ t ___. ___
4. Your **shin pads** are g r ___ ___ n. ___
5. Her **gloves** are y ___ l l ___ ___. ___
6. My **boots** are o r ___ ___ g ___. ___

A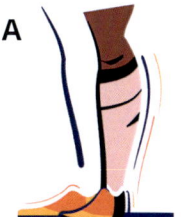
B
C
D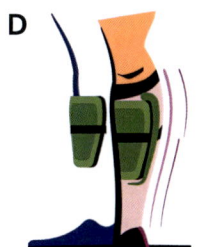
E
F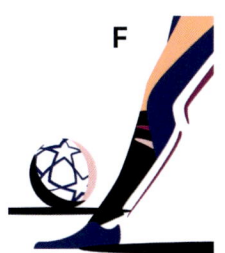

Exercise 2

> For **possessions (person + thing)**, we don't use *I/you/he/she*.

Complete the table below with the words from the box.

| your | our | his | her | ~~my~~ | their | whose | 's |

Person		+ Thing
who	→ _____	boots
I	→ *my*	boots
you	→ _____	shin pads
he	→ _____	shirt
she	→ _____	gloves
they	→ _____	tracksuit
we	→ _____	socks
Lucy	→ _____	shorts

Did you know…?
In American English, a **kit** is a *uniform*, football **boots** are called *cleats*, a football **shirt** is a *jersey* and **shin pads** are *shin guards*.

UNIT 4 | Football Kit

Part 2: Listening

Exercise 1

4.1 🔊 Harry and Jack are talking at the training ground.

Listen to the recording

a. Listen to the conversation. What are they talking about? (Circle) the correct answer.

  their football kit   the next match   their teammates

b. Listen again and complete the table.

Kit	Name
Shirt number ____	Harry
_____ number 7	Jack
	Miguel
	Josh and Luke
Armband	

Did you know?
At **big clubs** the players wear a **new shirt** for every game. After the game they give the shirts to charity or swap them with the opposition.

Part 3: Grammar

In the conversation, we heard Harry and Jack say:

"This **is** your **shirt**." (singular)
"These **are** your **short**s." (plural)

Look at how these words change:

Singular	Plural
This/That + **is** + a **shirt**/**tracksuit**.	These/Those + **are** + **short**s/**sock**s/**boot**s/**glove**s.

> See p86 for more about possessives.

Exercise 1

Are the following words **singular** or **plural**?

If the sentence is correct, put a ✓. If the sentence is wrong, correct it.

	✓	Correction
1. This are my **shirt**!		
2. Are these your **boots**?		
3. Whose **socks** is these?		
4. This are my **shin pads**!		
5. The **shirt** is Harry's!		

> **Nike or Adidas?**
>
> Players usually wear one **brand** of kit. For example, Haaland only wears Nike and Bellingham only wears Adidas. What **brand** are your boots? What **size** are they?

UNIT 4 | Football Kit

Part 4: Practice

Exercise 1

a. Look at the pictures and complete the sentences (**1–4**) using words from the box. You can use some words more than once.

LIAM   LUCA   SARAH   YOU

| 's | his | yours | mine | hers | theirs | ours | whose | Luca's |

1.	**Q:** Are these socks Liam _'s_ ? **A:** No, they aren't _____. They're _____.
2.	**Q:** Is this shirt Luca___? **A:** Yes, it's _____.
3.	**Q:** _____ gloves are these? **A:** They're Sarah___.
4.	**Q:** Are these shorts y_____? **A:** _____.

b. Now, use the same words from the box above to complete this table.

	Those are _____ boots.	Those boots are _____.
me	my	*mine*
you	your	
he		his
she	her	
they	their	

Part 5: Review

Exercise 1

a. Can you find and underline the errors in this paragraph?

Florian Wirtz are a football player. He from Germany. He a central midfielder. He plays corners and penalties. This is her shirt! Germany wear a white shirt, black shorts and orange socks.

b. Now write a paragraph about yourself! Include your personal details and a description of your football kit.

_____
_____
_____
_____
_____
_____
_____
_____
_____
_____
_____
_____
_____
_____
_____
_____
_____
_____

Lesson Goals

Vocabulary: Daily activities
Grammar: Present simple for routines
Skills: Describing daily life

UNIT 5
Daily Routine

What do professional footballers do all day, every day?
Are their lives the same as yours? This lesson looks at their
daily lives and helps you to talk about your own everyday life.

Part 1: Vocabulary

Exercise 1

a. Look at the word cloud to the right. Which of these **activities** do you do?

b. Choose words from the cloud to write under the pictures below **1–6**.

1. _____

2. _____

3. _____

4. _____

5. _____

6. _____

UNIT 5 | Daily Routine

5.1 **c.** Listen to 4 extracts. Write the activity (**A–F**) that you hear.

Listen to the recording

1. _C_
2. ___
3. ___
4. ___

d. Now rearrange these words to make the sentences you just heard.

1. up / wake / I / 7:30 / at _____
2. training / I / o'clock / 10 / at / have _____
3. o'clock / eat / 1 / at / lunch / I _____
4. 11:30 / to bed / I / at / go _____

e. Did you notice? Many activities in English use the verbs *go* or *have*. Look at these activities and write *go* or *have*.

1. _____ breakfast	2. _____ training	3. _____ a match	4. _____ free time
5. _____ to the gym	6. _____ to bed	7. _____ shopping	8. _____ home

f. Which of the activities above do you like? Which don't you like?

_____
_____
_____
_____
_____
_____

UNIT 5 | Daily Routine

Part 2: Listening

Exercise 1

🔊 **5.2** Jack and Harry are travelling to an away game. They're reading about their favourite players online. Listen to the conversation.
Where is Anderson from?

Listen to the recording

i. Brazil
ii. Spain
iii. England

Exercise 2

a. Listen again and complete the table.

Anderson's daily schedule	
Time	Activity
5am	
7am	
8am	_____ match
9am	_____ session
9:30am	_____ session
10am	

Home and away

Teams play **home** games at their ground, and **away** games at another team's ground.

Example: Locomotive London are **at home** in London. They're **away** at Manchester Athletic.

Not: ~~They are at away~~...

b. Is your life similar to Anderson's? Why or why not?

_____

_____

UNIT 5 | Daily Routine

Part 3: Grammar

In the conversation, we heard Jack and Harry using the **present simple**:

"... he **wakes** up at 5am."
"... he **goes** home at 10am."
"What **does** he **do**?"

We use the present simple to talk about our daily lives.

> See p87 for more about the present simple for routines.

Did you know?
Professional players eat and drink about **4,000 calories each day**. An average man only consumes about 2,500 calories and an average woman only 2,000 calories. Players often eat breakfast and lunch at the training ground to make sure they get the right foods.

Exercise 1

Complete the sentences in the present simple.

1. I _____ dinner at 9pm.
2. She _____ breakfast at the training ground.
3. They _____ to bed _____ midnight!
4. He _____ to training _____ the morning.
5. My team _____ go to the shopping mall at the weekend.
6. When do you _____ lunch?
7. What time _____ your best friend _____ home?

Part 4: Practice

Exercise 1

Complete the sentences so they are true for you!

1. I go to bed _____
2. In the mornings, I _____
3. On Fridays, I _____
4. My best friend goes _____
5. My teammates have _____

45

Exercise 2

A new player has just joined Locomotive London. They want to know more about life at the club, so they ask lots of questions.

Complete the conversation below with the words from the box. You can use some words more than once.

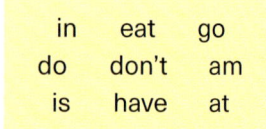

in	eat	go
do	don't	am
is	have	at

Harry: Hey, I'm Harry. What's your name?
Luca: My name 1._____ Luca! I 2._____ from Italy.
Harry: Nice to meet you, Luca! Welcome to Locomotive London!
Luca: Thanks! So, can I ask you some questions?
Harry: Sure!
Luca: What time do you 3._____ training here?
Harry: 4._____ the morning 5._____ 8:00am.
Luca: And where do you 6._____ breakfast?
Harry: At the training ground!
Luca: What 7._____ you do in the evening?
Harry: I 8._____ to the gym or 9._____ dinner with my friends. We 10._____ train in the evenings.
Luca: OK, great.
Harry: What about you? What do you 11._____ in the evenings?
Luca: I don't train, but I go to a restaurant for dinner.
Harry: Cool, let's go together sometime!

Exercise 3

a. It's your turn! First, match the questions (**1–3**) to the answers (**a–c**).

1. Do you have free time in the afternoon?
2. What do you do in your free time?
3. What time do we have training?

a. I use my phone and watch Netflix.
b. Yes, I do… after 2 o'clock.
c. We start at 10 o'clock.

b. Now, ask a friend the questions!

Part 5: Extra Time

Exercise 1

Write sentences about your daily life. Include 5 daily activities.

1. *I wake up at…* _____

2. _____

3. _____

4. _____

5. _____

REVIEW

Units 1–5

Exercise 1

Complete the sentences below (**1–5**) with the words from the box. Then match them to the positions on the pitch (**A–E**).

are
is
am
are
is

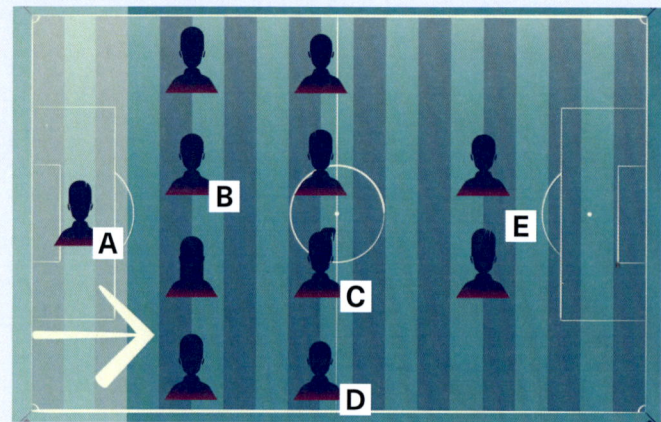

1. They ___ defenders. ___
2. He ___ a goalkeeper. ___
3. She ___ a forward. ___
4. I ___ a central midfielder. ___
5. You ___ a winger. ___

Exercise 2

Correct the mistakes in these sentences.

1. Eduardo take penalties for our team.
2. Ji So-Yun's boots is red.
3. Holland play in orange shirt.
4. Jamal Musiala don't take corners.
5. She shorts are blue.
6. Mia are from Canada.

Exercise 3

Match the questions (**1–5**) to the answers (**a–e**):

1. What time do you start training?
2. Whose black boots are these?
3. Where does she have lunch?
4. When do they have tactics sessions?
5. What time does he go to bed?

a. Around midnight.
b. At the training ground, at about midday.
c. I think they're Harry's!
d. Really early, at 6:30am!
e. Every Monday and Wednesday before lunch.

48

UNIT 6

The Body

Lesson Goals
Vocabulary: Parts of the body
Grammar: Can
Skills: Talking about injuries

This unit will help you talk about your body. Look at this picture of a physio talking to an injured player.

Where does it hurt? What are they saying?

Part 1: Vocabulary

Exercise 1

a. Label the **body parts** on the pictures below with the words from the box.

   back   arm   shoulder   chest   leg

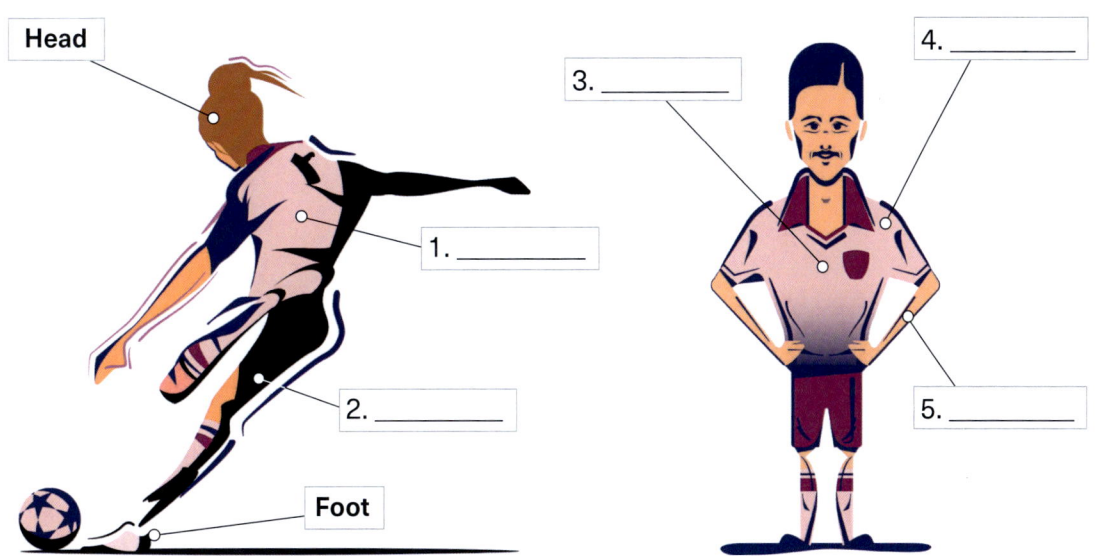

Head

1. _____
2. _____
Foot

3. _____
4. _____
5. _____

49

UNIT 6 | The Body

b. Complete the words to label the parts of the head.

Listen to the recording

 6.1

c. Listen to 5 extracts. Write the body part that you hear.

1. *eye*
2. _____
3. _____
4. _____
5. _____

h___ ___r
e___r
ey___
n___s___
m___ ___th
n___ ___k

Exercise 2

a. This picture shows parts of the body that are important in football. Do you know how to say them in your first language?

b. Rearrange the letters to complete the sentences.

1. I hurt my (klean) _____.
2. Does your (hight) _____ hurt?
3. It's my (ashmgintr) _____.
4. She injured her (nkee) _____.
5. Did he injure his (nhis) _____?

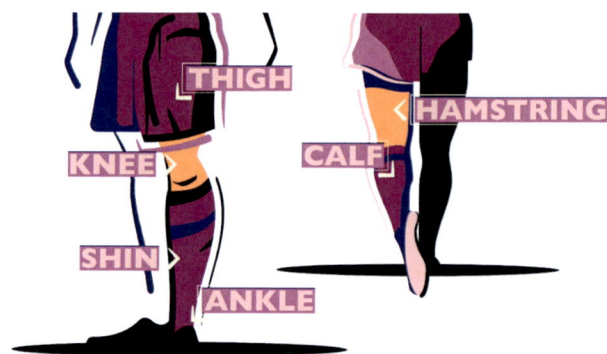

Exercise 3

Ask these questions to your partner:

- Which body parts have you injured?
- Which parts have you scored a goal with?
- Which do you use to pass?
- Which do you use to control the ball?

UNIT 6 | The Body

Part 2: Listening

6.2)) Exercise 1

Listen to the recording

Harry is watching a game from the bench. Jack is playing in the game.

a. Listen to the conversation. What happened to Harry?
  i. He hurt his leg.
  ii. He hurt his arm.
  iii. He hurt his head.

b. Listen again and match the pictures (**A–D**) to the expressions below (**1–4**).

1. "Where does it hurt?" ___
2. "Man on!" ___
3. "He has to **come off**!" ___
4. "**Substitution**! Miguel, you're **coming on**." ___

> **Top 5 injuries**
> Can you guess what the 5 most **common** football **injuries** are? Check your answers at the bottom of the page.

Top 5 injuries: 1. Hamstring 2. Ankle 3. Knee 4. Stomach (hernia) 5. Knee (ACL)

UNIT 6 | The Body

Part 3: Grammar

> In the conversation, we heard Jack ask Harry:
> "Can you walk?" (**can** + **person** + **verb**)
> We use **can** to talk about ability and possibility, so the answer is **yes** or **no**.
>
> The long form of **can't** is **cannot**.

See p88 for more about *can*.

Exercise 1

a. Look at the questions (**1–4**) and choose the correct answer.

1. Can you foul the referee?	i. No, I can't. That's a red card! ii. No, I don't. iii. Yes, I can.
2. Can defenders foul forwards in the box?	i. No, they can't. ii. No, they can't. That's a penalty. iii. No, they don't.
3. Can goalkeepers use their hands?	i. Yes, they do. ii. Yes, they can.
4. Can the coach take a free kick?	No, he _____.

b. Rearrange the words to make questions. Then write the answers.

Example: wingers/cross/can/the/ball
      <u>Can wingers cross the ball</u>? <u>Yes, they can</u>.

1. use/forwards/can/their/hands
_____? _____.

2. pass/midfielders/can
_____? _____.

3. referees/tackle/can
_____? _____.

4. Rodrygo/play/does/for/Mexico
_____? _____.

5. in/can/you/play/midfield
_____? _____.

UNIT 6 | The Body

Part 4: Practice

Exercise 1

Look at the pictures and complete the conversations.

Example:

Harry: Jack! __Man__ on!
Jack: Ouch! My leg!
Physio: Where does it __hurt__?
Jack: Here! __My__ knee.

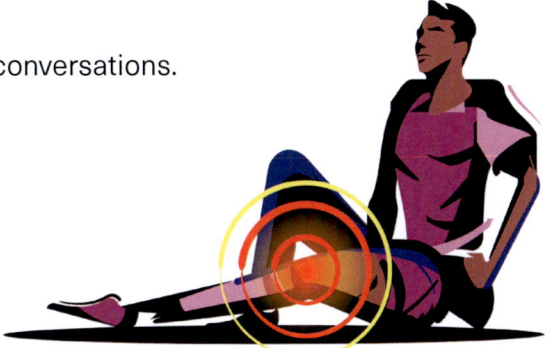

1. **A:** _____ does it hurt?
   B: My _____.

2. **A:** Are you OK?
   B: No, it's my _____.
   A: _____ you carry on?
   B: No, I can't. I think I have to _____ off.

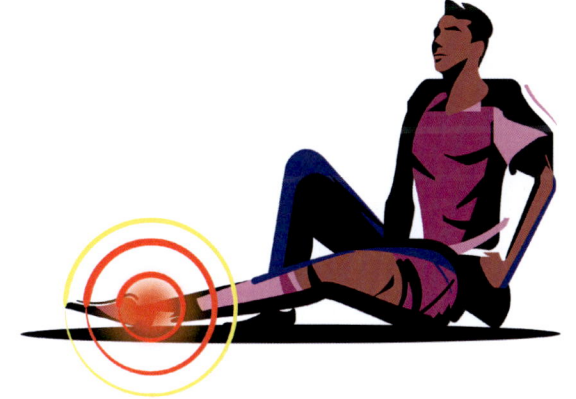

3. **A:** Where _____ it hurt?
   B: My _____.
   A: _____ this hurt?
   B: Ouch! Yes, it _____.

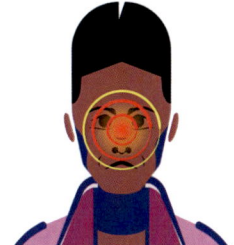

UNIT 6 | The Body

Exercise 2

Correct the 5 mistakes in this conversation.

Jack: Harry! Man in!
Harry: Ouch! My leg!
Physio: Is you OK, Harry?
Harry: No, my knee hurt!
Physio: Do this hurt?
Harry: Yes! Yes!
Physio: OK, you have to come on!

> **Did you know?**
> The fastest ever substitution was after 1 minute, during a Norwegian First Division game between Bryne and Tromsdalen in 2006. The player wasn't even injured!

Part 5: Extra Time

Exercise 1

You are going to interview your partner for the *Footballers Around the World* website.

Prepare a list of 8 questions, including 4 **wh-** questions (**1–4**) and 4 **yes/no** questions (**5–8**). Then interview your partner. Make sure you write down your partner's answers!

Questions	Answers
1. What's your name?	
2.	
3.	
4.	
5. Can you play midfield?	
6.	
7.	
8.	

UNIT 7

Lesson Goals

Vocabulary: Physical attributes
Grammar: *Be* + adjective / football expressions
Skills: Choosing a player

Describing Players

What do your favourite players **look like**? Are they big or small?
How about you? In this lesson, you'll learn how to describe what players look like and how they play the game.

Part 1: Vocabulary

Exercise 1

Look at the pictures below. Make opposite pairs to describe the pictures with the words from the box.

> fast   short   big   strong   overweight

slow ← → _____   _____ ← → slim   tall ← → _____

small ← → _____   weak ← → _____

> **Captain fantastic**
>
> **Captains** are leaders. They work hard and are respected on and off the pitch. Can you think of any famous captains?

55

UNIT 7 | Describing Players

Exercise 2

Rearrange these words to make sentences.

1. is/he/fast/winger/a _____
2. strong/she/a/is/defender _____
3. are/they/tall/midfielders _____
4. he/short/is/and/weak/a/goalkeeper _____
5. weak/forward/is/a/he _____

Exercise 3

a. Match the words (**1–5**) to the pictures (**A–E**).

1. left-footed ___
2. right-footed ___
3. good in the air ___
4. good on the ball ___
5. skilful ___

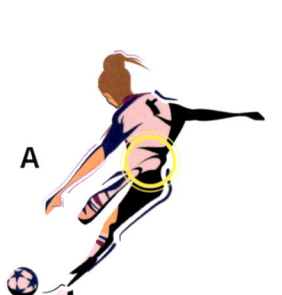

A

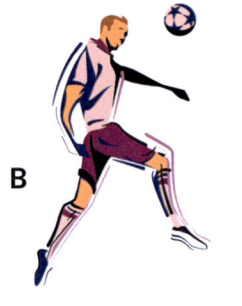

B

C

D

E

b. Which words describe your favourite players?

Part 2: Listening

Listen to the recording

7.1 🔊 **Exercise 1**

Harry and Jack are talking to each other after their last game.

a. Listen to the conversation. Why can't Harry play in the next game?

 i. His knee hurts.
 ii. He injured his hamstring.
 iii. His right foot hurts.

UNIT 7 | Describing Players

b. Harry and Jack talk about two other Locomotive London players, Miguel and Luca. Listen again and tick (✓) the physical attributes of each player.

Miguel	Luca
Short	Fast
Fast ✓	Two-footed
Strong	Tall
Good on the ball	Strong ✓
Left-footed	Skilful

> **Football fact**
> Approximately 25% of players are **left-footed**, and only 2% are **two-footed**.

c. What famous players are similar to Miguel and Luca?

Part 3: Grammar

> We can describe players using these 3 ways:
>
> "He's very **good**!" → be (**is**) + adjective (**good**)
> "He's a very **good player**." → be (**is**) + adjective (**good**) + noun (**player**)
> "He's very **good on the ball**." → be (**is**) + expression (**good on the ball**)

> See p89 for more about about *be* + adjective / expression.

57

UNIT 7 | Describing Players

Exercise 1

Complete the sentences below with the words from the box.

> forward   not   is   tall   are

1. He _____ a very fast winger.
2. They're so _____.
3. She is _____ a slow forward.
4. _____ they strong defenders?
5. I'm a really good _____.

Exercise 2

Correct the mistakes in these sentences.

1. He're a very fast winger.
2. They're very strongs defenders.
3. She's weak a goalkeeper.
4. My teammates is so good at football!

What a goal!

It's also important to describe goals and shots. First, label the parts of the goal.

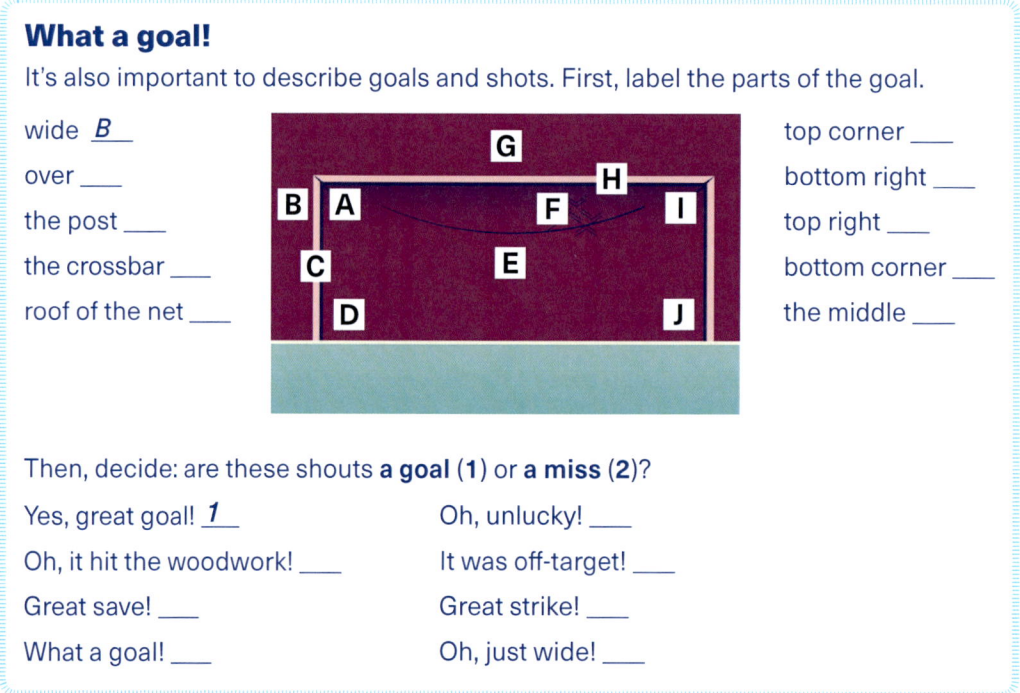

wide *B*
over ___
the post ___
the crossbar ___
roof of the net ___

top corner ___
bottom right ___
top right ___
bottom corner ___
the middle ___

Then, decide: are these shouts **a goal (1)** or **a miss (2)**?

Yes, great goal! *1*
Oh, it hit the woodwork! ___
Great save! ___
What a goal! ___

Oh, unlucky! ___
It was off-target! ___
Great strike! ___
Oh, just wide! ___

UNIT 7 | Describing Players

Part 4: Practice

Exercise 1

Match the players (**A–D**) to the descriptions (**1–4**).

  A. ~~Cubarsí~~
  B. Luca
  C. Miguel
  D. Vinicius

1. He's a tall, skilful, two-footed defender. ___
2. He's a fast, left-footed winger. ___
3. He's a very fast, two-footed, skilful forward who dribbles very well. ___
4. He's a tall, strong centre back who's a leader and good on the ball. _A_

Exercise 2

There's space for only 1 of these defenders in the Locomotive, London team for the next game. Who should start? Why?

A
NAME   TAKA
NATIONALITY   JAPANESE
AGE   24 YEARS OLD
POSITION   FULL BACK
ATTRIBUTES
FAST, SHORT, RIGHT-FOOTED, TAKES FREE KICKS

B
NAME   JACK
NATIONALITY   ENGLISH
AGE   21 YEARS OLD
POSITION   CENTRE BACK
ATTRIBUTES
FAST, BIG, A LEADER, LEFT-FOOTED

C
NAME   LUCA
NATIONALITY   ITALIAN
AGE   23 YEARS OLD
POSITION   CENTRE BACK
ATTRIBUTES
TALL, STRONG, TWO-FOOTED

D
NAME   HARRY
NATIONALITY   ENGLISH
AGE   21 YEARS OLD
POSITION   DEFENDER / MIDFIELDER
ATTRIBUTES
SLOW, WEAK, TALL, FOULS A LOT

UNIT 7 | Describing Players

Part 5: Speaking and Writing

Exercise 1

Quiz

a. Think of a famous player and write a description of him/her. Don't write the name! But do include the following:
- Nationality
- Age
- Position
- Physical attributes

b. Now read your description to a partner. Can they guess who it is?

UNIT 8

Playing in a Game

Lesson Goals
Vocabulary: In-game shouts
Grammar: Imperatives
Skills: Talking in a game

In a game, you hear many different **shouts** from coaches, teammates and fans. What **shouts** do you hear in your games? In this lesson, you'll learn some of the shouts used in games and training.

Part 1: Vocabulary

Exercise 1

a. Match the **shouts** (**1–12**) to the pictures (**A–L**).

1. Clear it! ___
2. Keep the ball! ___

3. Play it long! ___
4. Play it short! ___

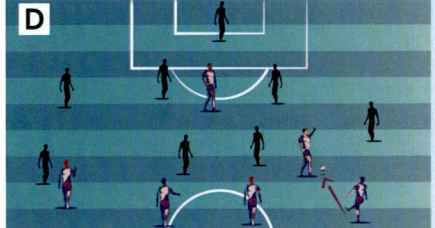

5. Man on! ___
6. Time! ___

UNIT 8 | Playing in a Game

7. Get tight! ___
8. Drop off! ___

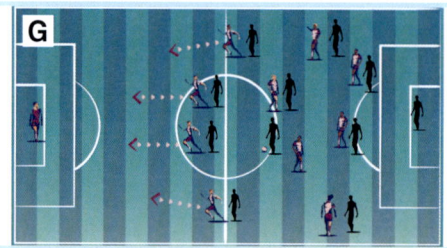

9. Push up! ___
10. Hold the line! ___

11. Switch it! ___
12. Shoot! ___

b. What shouts do you have in your first language? Are they the same?

8.1 🔊 **Exercise 2**

Listen to the recording

Listen to these extracts from a game. Choose the correct shouts from Exercise 1 and write them below.

Example: "Come on, mark up! Harry, you're on number 7."

1. *Mark up!* _____
2. _____
3. _____
4. _____

Set pieces

When defending set pieces like free kicks and corners, you'll hear **"Mark up!"** This means you should get tight and mark your player.

UNIT 8 | Playing in a Game

Exercise 3

Match the situations (**1–4**) to the shouts (**a–d**).

Situation	Shout
1. You want all the defenders to go to the halfway line.	a. Play it long!
2. It's the 94th minute. You're winning 1–0. The ball comes to a defender in your box.	b. Shoot!
3. You want the goalkeeper to kick it to the centre forward.	c. Clear it!
4. The forward has the ball in the opponents' box.	d. Push up!

Part 2: Listening

8.2))) Exercise 1

Harry and Jack are watching a game from the bench.

a. Listen to the conversation. How do Harry and Jack feel about the game?

   i. Positive ☺   ii. Negative ☹   iii. They don't care 😐

Listen to the recording

b. Harry and Jack shout at their team. First look at the pictures (**A–H**) and label them with the shouts, then listen again and order them (**1–8**).

A. *Get tight!* 2
B. _____ __

C. _____ __
D. *Mark up!* 1

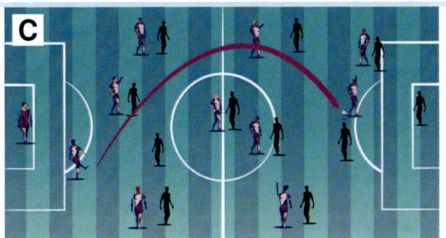

UNIT 8 | Playing in a Game

E. _____ __
F. _____ __

G. _____ __
H. _____ __

c. Match the new shouts from the listening (**1–3**) to the pictures (**I–J**).

1. Get goal-side! ___
2. Easy ball! ___
3. Play it to feet! ___

Exercise 2

Which shouts do you think are most important? Why?

Part 3: Grammar

Exercise 1

Complete the shouts.

1. Get _____ -side!
2. _____ play it long!
3. Switch _____ !
4. Clear _____ !
5. Man _____ !

> In the conversation, we heard Harry say:
>   "Get goal-side!"   "Don't drop off!"
>
> These are examples of **imperatives**.
> We use **imperatives** to give commands – or shouts.

See p90 for more about imperatives.

UNIT 8 | Playing in a Game

Exercise 2

Correct the mistakes in these shouts.

1. Mark down!
2. Men on!
3. Clear them!
4. Switch off!
5. Easy Jack!
6. Holding the line!

> **Ball game**
>
> We heard that Miguel is "good on the **ball**". In football there are many expressions with **ball**. Look at the expressions (**1–6**) below and decide when you say them (**A–C**).
>
> A: Someone does a good pass.
> B: Someone does a bad pass.
> C: You want a throw-in or corner.
>
> 1. What a ball! ___   2. Nice ball! ___   3. Poor ball! ___
> 4. Great ball! ___   5. Good ball! ___   6. Our ball! ___

Part 4: Practice

Exercise 1

Write a shout for each situation.

1. You're defending a corner.		*Mark up!*
2. There are many players on the right, but the left winger is in lots of space.		
3. You're defending a free kick near your box. You don't want the defence to go near the goal.		
4. The ball is in your half, but your fast centre forward is standing next to a slow centre back.		

UNIT 8 | Playing in a Game

Exercise 2

Locomotive London will play against Manchester Athletic next week, the best team in the league! Here's a profile of their best player, **Sam Smith**. Read the profile and then complete the tactical report with the words in the box.

well
isn't
is
mark
onside
on
off
hold

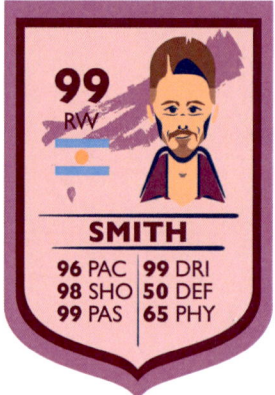

Tactical Report for Sam Smith

Sam 1. _____ a very good player. He's right-footed and very fast. He's very good 2. _____ the ball and reads the game 3. _____. He 4. _____ very tall or strong, but he's a very skilful player. The defence should 5. _____ him tightly, but not 6. _____ a high line because he's too fast. It's very important to stay 7. _____ and drop 8. _____ if he dribbles the ball.

Exercise 3

a. Write a tactical report for Mbappé, de Ligt or another player you know well.

_____
_____
_____
_____
_____
_____
_____

> **Video games**
> Some video games use abbreviations – short words – to describe players.
> **PAC** = pace (speed)
> **DRI** = dribbling
> **SHO** = shooting
> **DEF** = defending
> **PAS** = passing
> **PHY** = physical (height, strength)

b. Show the report to your partner. Do they agree with your advice?

Lesson Goals

Vocabulary: Midfield actions
Grammar: Past simple
Skills: Describing events after the game

UNIT 9
After the Game

Think about your last game: Did you win? Why were your team good or bad? In Unit 2, we talked about **football actions**. In this lesson, you'll learn more **actions** and how to talk about what happened in a game you played in or watched.

Part 1: Vocabulary

Exercise 1

Which of these words do you remember from Units 1–8? Circle any words you don't know.

UNIT 9 | After the Game

Exercise 2

a. Match sentences (**1–4**) to the pictures (**A–D**).

1. She switched it. ___
2. He squared it. ___
3. He headed it. ___
4. He dribbled it. ___

b. Match sentences (**1–4**) to the pictures (**A–D**).

1. He created a chance. ___
2. She scored a penalty. ___
3. He passed to the midfielder. ___
4. We pressed the defence. ___

c. Which of these actions did you do in your last game?

UNIT 9 | After the Game

Exercise 3

All the verbs in Exercise 2 have **-ed** at the end. This is how we talk about actions that happened in the **past**. This is called the **past simple** and there are 2 types of verbs: regular and irregular.

Regular (-ed)	Irregular
score – scor**ed**	eat – ate
head – head**ed**	go – went
pass – pass**ed**	wake up – woke up

See p95 for more irregular verbs.

See p91 for more about the past simple.

Can you find the **only word** from Exercise 1 that is irregular?

Exercise 4

Pronunciation

We say verbs ending in **-ed** in 3 ways: /d/, /t/ or /ɪd/. Put the words below into the correct column.

squared   switched   created   pressed   dribbled

/d/	/t/	/ɪd/
scored	*passed*	*headed*

The foot

We use 5 parts of the foot in football:

1. The sole
2. The laces
3. The inside
4. The outside
5. The toes

Which part do you use the most for these actions?

- Goal kick ___
- Stop the ball ___
- Dribble ___
- Cross ___

UNIT 9 | After the Game

Part 2: Listening

9.1 🔊 Exercise 1

Harry and Jack are listening to Head Coach Joe talk about their last game.

Listen to the recording

a. Listen to the conversation. How did Joe feel?

   i. happy ☺
   ii. angry 😠
   iii. sad ☹

b. Listen again. Complete the gaps in the sentences with words from the box.

| passed   were   was   score   didn't |

1. We _____ too slow.
2. Guys, your passing _____ too slow.
3. That's why we didn't _____!
4. Why _____ you pass, Jack?
5. They _____ the ball really well.

c. Is Joe the same as your coach or manager?
What does your coach or manager say when you lose?

UNIT 9 | After the Game

Part 3: Grammar

> In the conversation, Head Coach Joe said:
>   "We **were** too slow!"   "Your passing **was** too slow!"
> **Was** and **were** are from the irregular verb **be** (*am/is/are*).
> Look how the verb changes when talking about the past:
>   I ~~am~~ **was** fast.   He ~~is~~ **was** slow.   They ~~are~~ **were** good in the air.

Exercise 1

Change these sentences so they talk about **past** actions.

See p91 for more about the past simple.

Example:
He's really good on the ball. → _He was really good on the ball._

1. She's so strong. _____
2. They're quite slow on the counterattack. _____
3. He isn't a top goal-scorer. _____
4. She's an international defender. _____

> In the conversation, Joe said:
>   "They **passed** the ball really well!"
>   "Why **didn't** you **pass**, Jack?"
> To make a **question** (or **negative** sentence) about the past, we use
> ***did(n't)*** + **verb**.

Exercise 2

Complete the sentences below with the words from the box.

| scored | were | was | cleared | tackled | didn't | did |

1. They _____ 3 goals before half-time!
2. She _____ the ball off the line!
3. It _____ a terrible game, we lost 5–nil!
4. Why _____ you shoot? You were only 6 yards out!
5. Brazil _____ the best team in the 2002 World Cup.
6. _____ you watch the game? It was amazing! 4–3 to Locomotive!
7. He _____ the forward, but the referee gave a penalty!

Exercise 3

Correct the past simple mistakes in these sentences.

1. He were a great player!
2. He don't square the ball!
3. She didn't passed the ball!
4. It is a brilliant game, just brilliant!
5. They was a terrible team!

Part 4: Practice

Exercise 1

Write sentences to describe the pictures.

Example:

Central midfielder Winger Forward

The central midfielder passed to the winger, then he crossed it and the forward headed the ball into the goal.

Winger Full back Midfielder

1. _____
_____

UNIT 9 | After the Game

Centre back Full back Forward

2. _____
   _____

 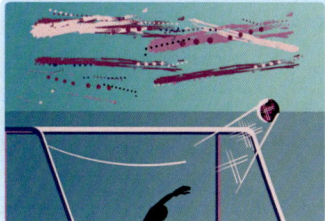

Defender Winger Forward

3. _____
   _____

Let's play!

In football, there are many collocations with the word **play**. For example, in Unit 8 we saw **play** it long and **play** it short. Match these types of pass (**1–3**) to the pictures (**A–C**).

1. Play a through-ball.
   ___

2. Play it over the top.
   ___

3. Play a one-two.
   ___

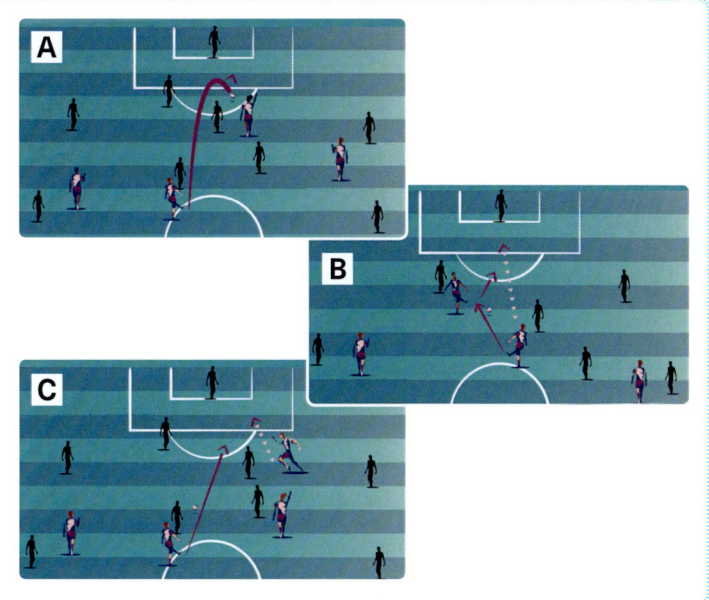

73

UNIT 9 | After the Game

Exercise 2

Complete the match report below with the words from the box.

> was   scored   were   crossed   was   played   penalty   missed

Locomotive London ¹·_____ Manchester Athletic yesterday. The score ²·_____ 3–0 to Locomotive, and Jack ³·_____ an incredible hat-trick! The best goal ⁴·_____ a volley from outside the box. He also scored a ⁵·_____ and a close-range finish after Harry ⁶·_____ the ball. Head Coach Joe was very happy, and the fans ⁷·_____ very happy too, especially after Manchester ⁸·_____ a penalty in injury time!

Part 5: Speaking and Writing

Exercise 1

a. Choose a favourite goal or match. Write about it! When was the match? Who played? What happened?

_____
_____
_____
_____
_____
_____
_____
_____
_____
_____

b. Read your match report to your partner.

Lesson Goals

Vocabulary: Standings and results
Grammar: Future tense
Skills: Describing fixtures and results

UNIT 10

Fixtures and Results

What was the **result** of your last game? Did you win? What about your next **fixtures**? Do you think you will win?

In this lesson, you'll learn how to talk about the scores of games you played in (**results**) and the games you will play in the future (**fixtures**)!

Part 1: Vocabulary

Exercise 1

Look at these football results. Choose the correct option for each result.

1. FRANCE 2–1 ITALY
    i. France beat Italy two–one.
    ii. France beat Italy two to one.
    iii. France drew two–one.

2. CHINA 3–3 JAPAN
    i. China drew three to three.
    ii. China beat Japan three-all.
    iii. China drew three-all.

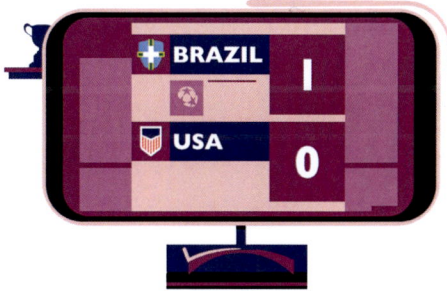

3. BRAZIL 1–0 USA
    i. Brazil won one–nil.
    ii. Brazil lost one–nil.
    iii. Brazil win one–nil.

4. ENGLAND 1–2 GERMANY
    i. England lost to Germany two–one.
    ii. England lose to Germany two and one.
    iii. England lost Germany two to one.

75

UNIT 10 | Fixtures and Results

> **Grammar note**
> The examples above are talking about the **past**. *Won*, *drew* and *lost* are **irregular verbs** (see Unit 9). How do you say them in the **present**?
>
> _____ → won
> _____ → drew
> _____ → lost
>
> See p95 for more irregular verbs.
>
> **Did you notice?**
> We say: "Brazil **won** one–nil." Not: ~~Brazil beat one nil.~~
> "Brazil **beat the USA** one–nil." Not: ~~Brazil won the USA one nil.~~
>
> Look at the examples in Exercise 1. How do you use *lost* and *lost to*?

Exercise 2

Complete the sentences and say the results.

1. Corinthians _____ São Paulo two–_____.

2. Real Madrid and Barcelona _____ three–_____.

3. Fenerbahçe _____ Galatasary one–_____.

4. Juventus _____ two–one.

UNIT 10 | Fixtures and Results

Exercise 3

What are your team's latest results? What about the team you support?

_____
_____
_____

Exercise 4

Read the league table, then complete the sentences below with the words from the box.

LEAGUE TABLE

P	TEAM	PTS
1	MANCHESTER ATHLETIC	67
2	LIVERPOOL CITY	66
3	LOCOMOTIVE LONDON	63
4	BRISTOL F.C	61
5	BIRMINGHAM WANDERERS	54
6	NEWCASTLE TOWN	54
7	CARDIFF CENTRAL	32

> top   bottom   second   third   fourth   in   of   have

1. Manchester Athletic are _____ of the league with 67 points.
2. Liverpool City are _____.
3. Locomotive London _____ 63 points. They're _____.
4. Cardiff Central are _____ _____ the league.
5. Newcastle Town are _____ sixth.
6. Bristol FC are _____ in the league.

Exercise 5

Where is your team in the league?
What about the team you support?

Did you notice?
We say *top of* and *bottom of* the league, but *second/third/fourth/fifth in* the league.

UNIT 10 | Fixtures and Results

Part 2: Listening

10.1 🔊 Exercise 1

Harry and Jack are talking about the fixture list.

Listen to the recording

a. Listen to the conversation and answer the questions.

1. How do Harry and Jack feel about their last game?
   i. Happy   ☺
   ii. Disappointed   ☹

2. How do Harry and Jack feel about their next game?
   i. Positive   ☺
   ii. Worried   ☹

b. Listen again and complete the table with the results you hear.

Team	Score	Score	Team
Locomotive London			Liverpool City
Bristol FC			Manchester Athletic
Newcastle Town			Cardiff Central

Exercise 2

Do you think Locomotive London will win their next game? Why or why not?

UNIT 10 | Fixtures and Results

Part 3: Grammar

In the conversation, we heard:

"Who **are** we play**ing**?" "We **are** play**ing** Manchester next Saturday!"
"Who do you think **will** win?" "I think we **will** win!"

These sentences are about **the future**.
We use **be + -ing** verb for future **fixtures and plans**.
We use **will + verb** for **predictions**.

The short form of **will** is **'ll**.
The short form of **will not** is **won't**.

See p93 for more about the future tense.

Exercise 1

Rearrange these words to make sentences. Then write **F** (for fixtures) or **P** (for predictions). Sometimes more than one option is possible.

Sentence	F/P
1. Liverpool/Sunday/we're/playing/next	
2. think/Manchester/I/will/win	
3. Bristol/Newcastle/tomorrow/are/playing	
4. lose/Cardiff/think/will/I	
5. on/Birmingham/playing/Wednesday/are/against/Manchester	

Home or away?

Home advantage is very important in football. The **home team wins** 50% of their matches. They **draw** 20% of matches and **lose** only 30%.

UNIT 10 | Fixtures and Results

Exercise 2

Correct the mistakes in these sentences. Use Part 1: Vocabulary to help you!

1. I think we'll ~~won~~ our next game! ___win___
2. We're playing in home tomorrow. _____
3. I think Real Madrid draw next week. _____
4. Tottenham are play Arsenal on Saturday! _____
5. I think the game will be zero–zero. _____

Part 4: Practice

Exercise 1

Look at these situations. What do you think will happen next?

Situation		Prediction
	The goalkeeper is sent off	*I think…*
	A player is injured	
	A free kick near the goal	
	A penalty	

UNIT 10 | Fixtures and Results

Exercise 2

Complete the football blog below with the words from the box.

| will | thinks | won | They're | away | on | home | lose | beat |

Locomotive London have a very busy schedule this week. 1._____ playing Liverpool City 2._____ Saturday, which I think 3._____ be a very good game because both teams love to attack. Last week, Liverpool 4._____ Bristol 4–0 and Locomotive 5._____ by 3 goals! On Wednesday, Locomotive play at 6._____ against Bristol, a game everyone 7._____ Locomotive will win. The following Sunday, Locomotive play 8._____ at Manchester Athletic – I think they'll 9._____ because Manchester are unbeaten this season at home, but what about you? Leave your predictions below!

REVIEW

Units 6–10

Exercise 1

Match the questions (**1–5**) to the answers (**a–e**).

1. Can you play on?
2. Can you take corners from the right?
3. Can they win the derby?
4. Can she play on Sunday?
5. Can you play in midfield?

a. Yes, I think they can!
b. No, I can't – I'm a goalkeeper.
c. No, I can't – I can't move my ankle.
d. No, she pulled her hamstring.
e. Yes, I can – and from the left, too!

Exercise 2

Correct the **past simple** mistakes in these sentences.

1. Real Madrid winned last week against Manchester United.
2. Haaland were incredible yesterday – two goals and an assist, amazing!
3. What you did last week? Did you train a lot?
4. I was surprised Chelsea didn't lost the final.
5. When is our tactics session, did I miss it?

Exercise 3

Complete the sentences below with the words from the box.

| away | will | drew | top | think |

1. Locomotive London are _____ of the league with 64 points.
2. I _____ Bayern Munich will win the Champions League!
3. Inter are playing the _____ leg next week.
4. Tottenham _____ away with Valencia.
5. Who do you think _____ win the World Cup?

Grammar Reference

UNIT 1
Present simple *be*

Positive and negative

The verb *be* has 3 forms in the present simple: *am*, *is* and *are*. We make negatives by adding *not* after *be*.

Singular			Plural		
I	am		we	are	
you	are	(not)	you	are	(not)
he / she / it	is		they	are	

Contractions

We often join words together. These joined words are called **contractions**.

Positive (+)		Negative (−)	
I am	→ I'm	I am not	→ I'm not
you are	→ you're	you are not	→ you aren't / you're not
he is	→ he's	he is not	→ he isn't / he's not
she is	→ she's	she is not	→ she isn't / she's not
it is	→ it's	it is not	→ it isn't / it's not
we are	→ we're	we are not	→ we aren't / we're not
they are	→ they're	they are not	→ they aren't / they're not

I'm a midfielder. You're a striker. It's an important match. They're a good team.
I'm not the coach. You aren't a defender. She isn't Brazilian. They're not here yet.

Questions

We make questions by putting the verb *be* before the subject (e.g. *I*, *she*).
We put question words (e.g. *What, Where, Who, When, Why*) at the beginning.

(Question word)	Be	Subject	(Rest of question)
	Am	I	a good player?
	Are	you	ready?
What	is	your name?	
Where	are	the other players?	
Why	are	they	late?
When	is	the match?	

83

We can also use contractions with question words:
What + is = What's; Where + is = Where's, etc.

> *What's your name? Where's she from?*
> *When's the match?*

Short answers
When somebody asks a *yes*/*no* question, we often answer with a short answer.

	Positive (+)			Negative (−)	
Yes,	I	am.	No,	I'm	not.
	you / we / they	are.		you / we / they	aren't.
	he / she / it	is.		he / she / it	isn't.

A: *Are you Brazilian?* **B:** *Yes, I am. / No, I'm not.*
A: *Are they defenders?* **B:** *Yes, they are. / No, they aren't.*

UNIT 2

Present simple (+/−)
We use the present simple to talk about:

1. **States** that are true now or always.
   I love football. We want to win the match. She knows the rules.
   State verbs include *like*, *love*, *want*, *know*, *cost*, *understand*, *agree* and *have*.

2. **Actions** that happen always, often, sometimes or never.
   She plays in attack. (= she always plays in that position)
   You often score goals. They sometimes head the ball.

Positive (+)
For most verbs, the present simple is the same as the infinitive. For *he/she/it*, add *-s*.
Two verbs (*be* and *have*) are irregular.

I / you / we / they	play know save have	he / she / it	play**s** know**s** save**s** ha**s**

Spelling: adding *-s* for *he/she/it*
When a verb ends in *-o, -s, -sh, -ch* or *-x*, add *-es*.

I do / go / pass / push / watch / relax. → *She does / goes / passes / pushes / watches / relaxes.*

When a verb ends in a consonant (e.g. *d, l, r*) + *y*, change the *-y* to *-ies*.

I study / fly / try. → *He studies / flies / tries.*

> **Did you know?**
> *Never* has a negative meaning, but we use it in positive sentences.
>
> *We never win big matches!* (**Not:** ~~We never don't win~~ …)

But when a verb ends in a vowel (*a, e, i, o, u*) + *y*, just add *-s*.

I pl<u>ay</u> / enj<u>oy</u> / b<u>uy</u>. → She play<u>s</u> / enjoy<u>s</u> / buy<u>s</u>.

Don't forget!
Don't add *-s* to the verb after *doesn't*!

Negative (−)
We make negatives by adding *don't* (= *do not*) or *doesn't* (= *does not*) before the verb.

I / you / we / they	don't	play know save have	he / she / it	doesn't	play know save have

UNIT 3
Present simple (?)
Yes/no questions
We make *yes/no* questions by adding *do* or *does* before the subject.

Positive		
Subject	**Verb**	
I You We They	love like hate	football
He She It	loves likes hates	

Question			
Do/does	**Subject**	**Verb**	
Do	I you we they	love like hate	football?
Does	he she it		

Short answers
When somebody asks a *yes/no* question, we often answer with a short answer.

Don't forget!
In questions, don't add *-s* to the verb after *does*!
Does she know the rules?
(**Not:** ~~*Does she knows ...?*~~)

	Positive (+)			Negative (−)	
Yes,	I / you / we / they	do.	No,	I / you / we / they	don't.
	he / she / it	does.		he / she / it	doesn't.

A: *Do you take corners?*   **B:** *Yes, I do. / No, I don't.*
A: *Does it hurt when you head the ball?*   **B:** *Yes, it does. / No, it doesn't.*

Wh- questions

Wh- questions start with question words like *who*, *what*, *where*, *when*, *why* and *how*, or phrases like *what time*, *how often* or *which position*.

Question word/phrase	Do/does	Subject		Verb	
Where	does	she		play?	
Why	do	they	always	win?	
What time	does	your training		start	on Tuesdays?
Which position	do	you		play	in?

Subject questions

When you ask about the subject, the word order is the same as in a positive sentence. Don't add *do/does*.

	Positive				Subject question		
Subject	Verb			Question word/phrase	Verb		
Emma	passes	the most.	→	Who		passes	the most?
Liam	takes	penalties.		Which player		takes	penalties?
Something	happens	after a foul.		What		happens	after a foul?

UNIT 4

Possessives

Possessives with apostrophe + -s

We use possessives to show that something belongs to somebody. We usually do this by adding an apostrophe (') and -s after the person.

This ball belongs to Kevin. It's Kevin's ball. The ball is Kevin's.
These boots belong to the player in the red shirt. They're the player in the red shirt's boots.

> **Did you know?**
>
> When there's already an *-s* to show a plural (e.g. *the 3 defenders*), just add an apostrophe after the *-s*. Don't add another *-s*.
> *These shirts belong to the 3 defenders. They're the 3 defenders' shirts.*

Possessive determiners and possessive pronouns

We use possessive determiners (e.g. *my*) **before** a noun. We use possessive pronouns (e.g. *mine*) **instead of** a noun.

These socks belong to me. They're my socks. These socks are mine.

Personal pronoun	Possessive determiner	Possessive pronoun
I	They're **my** socks.	They're **mine**.
you	They're **your** socks.	They're **yours**.
he	They're **his** socks.	They're **his**.
she	They're **her** socks.	They're **hers**.
it	They're **its** socks.	–
we	They're **our** socks.	They're **ours**.
they	They're **their** socks.	They're **theirs**.
who	**Whose** socks are they?	**Whose** are these socks?

Singular and plural

We use singular forms (e.g. *a ball*, *a player*) for one person or thing, and plural forms (e.g. *balls*, *players*) for more than one person or thing.

We use *a* or *an* before a noun to show that it's singular. Use *a* before a consonant sound: *a ball, a goal*. Use *an* before a vowel sound: *an attacker, an open goal*.

We usually use *-s* after a noun to show that it's plural: *10 balls, 22 players, 2 attackers*.

This, that, these and those

We use *this* for something that's "here" (= near the speaker) and *that* for something that's "there" (= away from the speaker). The plural forms are *these* and *those*.

	Singular	Plural
"here"	this	these
"there"	that	those

This shirt (here) is red; that shirt (there) is blue.
These socks (here) are white; those socks (there) are green.

UNIT 5

Present simple for routines
We use the present simple to talk about our daily routines (= things we do every day).

Adverbs of frequency
We use adverbs of frequency to say how often something happens.

0% ◄···► 100%
never   not often   sometimes   often/usually   always

Most adverbs of frequency come after *be* and *not* (or *n't*), but before other verbs.

A: *You never pass to me.*   **B:** *You're never in the right place for me to pass to you!*

We usually lose our matches and it's usually my fault.
She doesn't always score a goal because she isn't always a striker.

Frequency expressions

We use frequency expressions to say **exactly** how often something happens.

I play football	every		morning / afternoon / evening. day. Sunday / Tuesday / Thursday. week. month.
	once twice three times ten times	a every	day. week. month.

Time expressions with prepositions

We use *at* with times: *at ten o'clock, at midnight*.

We use *on* for days: *on Tuesdays*.

We use *in* with parts of a day:
in the morning(s), in the afternoon(s), in the evening(s).
But we use *at* with *night*: *at night*.

We use *in* with months, seasons, years, etc.:
in July, in the spring, in 2023.

> **Did you know?**
> In British English, people say "**at** the weekend(s)". In American English, people say "**on** (the) weekend(s)".

UNIT 6

Can

Positive and negative

We use *can* to talk about ability, rules and permission. The negative form is *can't* (= *can + not*).

Positive (+)			Negative (−)		
I / you / he / she / it / we / they	can	play football.	I / you / he / she / it / we / they	can't	play football.

Ability: *I can't score a goal from the halfway line – it's too far!*
Rules: *The goalkeeper can use his or her hands, but the other players can't pick it up.*
Permission: *No, sorry, you can't play in attack today. We need you in defence.*

> **Don't forget!**
> With *can*, there's no *-s* for *he/she/it*: *He can play.*
> (**Not:** ~~He cans play.~~)
>
> There's no *to* after *can*:
> *We can't run fast.*
> (**Not:** ~~We can't to run fast.~~)

Questions

We make questions by putting the verb *can* before the subject.

(Question word/phrase)	Can/can't	Subject	Verb	
	Can	you	play	in goal?
Why	can't	I	keep	playing?
When	can	the match	start?	
Which positions	can	she	play	in?

Don't forget!
Subject questions have the same word order as positive sentences.
Lucy can dribble the ball the best. → *Which player can dribble the ball the best?*

Short answers

When somebody asks a question with *can*, we often answer with a short answer.

Positive (+)			Negative (–)		
Yes,	I / you / he / she / it / we / they	can.	No,	I / you / he / she / it / we / they	can't.

A: Can you move your arm?   **B:** Yes, I can. / No, I can't.
A: Can I take this corner, please?   **B:** Yes, you can. / No, you can't.

UNIT 7
Be + adjective/football expressions

Don't forget!
There are 3 forms of *be* in the present simple: *I am; you/we/they are; he/she/it is.*

Be + adjective
We often use *be* + adjective to describe somebody or something.

I'm tired. It's difficult. They're excellent.

You can use *very* or *really* to make the meaning of the adjective stronger. Use *quite* to make it weaker. Use *not very* to make it very weak.

strong ◄─────────────────────────────► **weak**
She's very/really good.   *She's good.*   *She's quite good.*   *She isn't very good.*

Be (+ adjective) + noun
We can also use *be* + noun to describe somebody or something. We can add 1 or more adjectives before the noun. We can add words like *very*, *really* and *quite* before the adjective.

He's a defender.   *He's a skilful, left-footed defender.*
He's a left-footed defender.   *He's a really skilful, left-footed defender.*

Grammar Reference

 Don't forget!
We use *a/an* to show that the noun is singular and *-s* to show it's plural.
They're defenders.
(**Not:** ~~They're a defenders.~~)

Did you know?
Opinion adjectives (e.g. *good*, *skilful*, *fast*, *tall*) come before fact adjectives (e.g. *right-footed*).
She's a good, two-footed midfielder.
(**Not:** ~~She's a two-footed good midfielder.~~)

Be + **adjective** + **expression**
We can sometimes add expressions after *be* + adjective.

Subject + *be*	Adjective	Expression
I'm	excellent	**on** the ball.
You're	good	**at** football / passing / defending.
She's	not bad	**with** her head / left foot.
He's	not very good	
	terrible	**in** the air / in attack / in midfield.

So **and** *such*
We can use *so* and *such* to make an adjective stronger. Use *so* when there's an adjective without a noun. Use *such* when there's an adjective and a noun.
He's so skilful. He's such a skilful player.

UNIT 8

Imperatives

Basic imperatives
We use imperatives to ask or tell other people what to do. They have the same form as the infinitive of the verb (e.g. *be*, *go*, *wait*).

Be careful!
Go back!
Wait for me!

Negative imperatives
Negative imperatives start with *don't*.

Don't touch the ball!
Don't tell me what to do!
Don't be so rude!

Polite imperatives
Imperatives sometimes sound rude. You can add *please* to make them sound more polite.

Please wait here.
Follow me, please.

Did you know?
You can also use *can* instead of an imperative to ask somebody to do something.
Can you come here, please?
Can you say that again, please?

Imperatives for more than one person

You can use a phrase like *you two*, *all of you* or *everybody* to make it clear that an imperative is for more than one person.

All of you be quiet!
OK, everybody listen to me.
Stop fighting, you two.

UNIT 9

Past simple

Be

The verb *be* has 2 forms in the past simple: *was* and *were*. The negative forms are *wasn't* (= was not) and *weren't* (= were not).

Positive (+)			Negative (−)		
I / He / She / It	was	good.	I / He / She / It	wasn't	good.
We / You / They	were		We / You / They	weren't	

It wasn't a good match. We were terrible.
The score was 4–0. All the players were sad.

To make a *yes/no* question, put *was/were* before the subject.

Question			Short answer		
Was	I / he / she / it	good?	Yes,	I / he / she / it	was.
			No,		wasn't.
Were	you / we / they	good?	Yes,	you / we / they	were.
			No,		weren't.

A: *Were you happy with the result?* **B:** *No, we weren't.*
A: *Was the referee fair?* **B:** *Yes, she was.*

To make a *wh-* question, put a question word or phrase before *was/were*.

What was the score? Why were the players sad?

Regular verbs

To make the past simple form of regular verbs, add *-ed*. To make the negative form, use *didn't* (= did not) + infinitive.

Positive (+)			Negative (−)			
I / You / He / She / It / We / They	played	well.	I / You / He / She / It / We / They	didn't	play	well.
	scored	a goal.			score	a goal.
	headed	the ball.			head	the ball.

To make a *yes/no* question, put *did* before the subject and put the infinitive after the subject.

Question				Short answer		
Did	I / you / he / she / it / we / they	play score	well? a goal?	Yes, No,	I / you / he / she / it / we / they	did. didn't.

Don't forget!
After *did* and *didn't*, the verb is in the infinitive, not the past simple:
Did you play well?
(**Not:** ~~Did you played well?~~)
We didn't play well.
(**Not:** ~~We didn't played well.~~)

To make a *wh-* question, put a question word or phrase before *did*.
Where did you play? Who did you play against? What time did the match start?

Don't forget!
Subject questions have the same word order as positive sentences.
Miguel scored a goal. → *Who scored a goal?*

Spelling regular verbs
For most regular verbs, add *-ed*.
head → *headed, miss* → *missed*

When the verb already ends in *-e*, just add *-d*.
save → *saved, agree* → *agreed*

When the verb ends in a consonant (e.g. *p, r*) + *-y*, change the *-y* to *-ied*.
copy → *copied, try* → *tried*

But when the verb ends in a vowel (*a, e, i, o, u*) + *-y*, just add *-ed*.
play → *played, enjoy* → *enjoyed*

When the verb ends in one vowel + one consonant, double the consonant.
plan → *planned, stop* → *stopped*

Irregular verbs

Many verbs are irregular in the past simple. That means you can't simply add -ed to make the past simple. You need to learn the past form. See page 95 for a list of irregular verbs.

We won the match.
She shot 3 times but didn't score!

UNIT 10

Future tense

Future tense (*will*)

We use *will* to make predictions about the future. The negative form is *won't* (= *will not*).

Positive (+)			Negative (−)		
I / You / He / She / It / We / They	will	win.	I / You / He / She / It / We / They	won't	win.

We often use contractions with *will*: *I'll* (= *I will*), *you'll, he'll, she'll, it'll, we'll, they'll*; *won't* (= *will not*).

We won't win. They'll probably beat us 10–0!

> **Did you know?**
> We often use the phrase *I don't think* to make negatives with *will*.
> *I don't think we'll win.*

To make a *yes/no* question, put *will* before the subject. To make a *wh-* question, put a question word or phrase before *will*.

Question			Short answer		
Will	I / you / he / she / it / we / they	win?	Yes, No,	I / you / he / she / it / we / they	will. won't.

A: *Will you score a goal?* **B:** *Yes, I will.*
How many goals will they score?

> **Did you know?**
> We often use the phrase *do you think* to make questions with *will*. When we use *do you think*, we put *will* after the subject.
> **A:** *Do you think you'll score a goal?*
> (**Not:** ~~Do you think will you score a goal?~~)
> **B:** *Yes, I do.* (**Not:** ~~Yes, I will.~~)
> *How many goals do you think they'll score?*

Be + -ing verb for future

We use a present form of the verb *be* + the *-ing* form of a verb (e.g. *playing*) to talk about future fixtures and plans.

I'm playing in goal tomorrow because our goalkeeper is injured.
We bought a new striker last week. She's starting with us tomorrow.
We aren't playing next week because it's a holiday weekend.
A: *Am I playing tomorrow?*   **B:** *Yes, you are. / No, you aren't.*
Who are we playing on Thursday?

Don't forget!
There are 3 forms of *be* in the present simple: *I am; you/we/they are; he/she/it is.*

Irregular Verbs

Infinitive	Past Simple	Past Participle	Infinitive	Past Simple	Past Participle
be	was / were	been	lose	lost	lost
beat	beat	beaten	make	made	made
become	became	become	mean	meant	meant
begin	began	begun	meet	met	met
bring	brought	brought	pay	paid	paid
buy	bought	bought	put	put	put
catch	caught	caught	read	read	read
choose	chose	chosen	ride	rode	ridden
come	came	come	run	ran	run
cost	cost	cost	say	said	said
do	did	done	see	saw	seen
draw	drew	drawn	sell	sold	sold
drink	drank	drunk	send	sent	sent
drive	drove	driven	shoot	shot	shot
eat	ate	eaten	sing	sang	sung
fall	fell	fallen	sit	sat	sat
feel	felt	felt	sleep	slept	slept
find	found	found	speak	spoke	spoken
fly	flew	flown	spend	spent	spent
forget	forgot	forgotten	stand	stood	stood
get	got	got	steal	stole	stolen
give	gave	given	swim	swam	swum
go	went	gone	take	took	taken
have	had	had	teach	taught	taught
hear	heard	heard	tell	told	told
hit	hit	hit	think	thought	thought
hold	held	held	throw	threw	thrown
hurt	hurt	hurt	understand	understood	understood
keep	kept	kept	wake	woke	woken
know	knew	known	wear	wore	worn
leave	left	left	win	won	won
let	let	let	write	wrote	written

Listening Scripts

UNIT 1
Track 1.1
Jack: Hey Harry, what's up?
Harry: Hey Jack! How are you?
Jack: Fine, you?
Harry: Great… but… Listen, who is that?
Jack: That's Miguel, the new player from Spain!
Harry: Wow, he's Spanish!
Jack: Yeah, he's really good!
Harry: Yeah? What position is he?
Jack: He's a midfielder, I think.
Harry: Oh no…
Jack: What's wrong, Harry?
Harry: Midfielder! I am a midfielder!
Jack: Relax, you're a very good player, Harry!
Harry: Thanks, Jack… but, uh, I think I will go and train now!
Jack: See you, Harry… and, uh, good luck!

UNIT 2
Track 2.1
Harry: Are you ready for this quiz, Jack?
Jack: Yes, sure! Let's go!
Harry: Great! Who is this player? He's a midfielder, he doesn't score many goals, but he creates many chances!
Jack: Umm…
Harry: His national team play in white… he has short hair. He passes the ball very well, but doesn't shoot a lot…
Jack: Ah, that's easy! He's from Germany, right? It's Florian Wirtz!
Harry: Correct, well done! Ready for the next one?
Jack: Yep!
Harry: OK, he is a winger, so he attacks a lot and he crosses a lot…
Jack: He sounds Brazilian!
Harry: No, he's Spanish… so he doesn't tackle a lot!
Jack: Nico Williams!
Harry: Close! But Williams tackles! This Spanish player doesn't tackle and he doesn't head the ball, but he scores goals and he is an amazing player!
Jack: Lamine Yamal!
Harry: Correct! OK, next! This player scores lots of goals with his head, scores a lot of goals with his body!
Jack: Easy! Vinicius Junior!
Harry: No, Vinicius doesn't head a lot of goals…
Jack: Umm… Haaland! Erling Haaland!
Harry: Yes! This is too easy – one more…
Jack: OK!
Harry: OK, who is this player? He plays in midfield… he doesn't score… or pass… or cross… or tackle… or head the ball… or…
Jack: Wait, what?!
Harry: It's you after lunch, Jack!

UNIT 3
Track 3.1
Joe: Right boys, listen up! Right, tactics for our next game. Because Miguel is injured, we have to change some things for tomorrow's game.
Jack: OK, Coach!
Joe: So, I'll talk about set pieces first. Jack, you take corners on the left.
Jack: From the left, got it.
Joe: And Harry, you take corners on the right.
Harry: The right? Yes, Coach!
Joe: I want you to switch for free kicks, OK? Jack, you take free kicks from the right.
Jack: Yes, no problem.
Joe: And Harry, you take free kicks from the left.
Harry: Yes, Coach. What else?
Joe: Jack, I want you to take penalties, OK?
Jack: Me, on penalties? Yes, of course!
Joe: Good. Any questions?
Boys: No, Coach!
Joe: Right, go and practise some corners – it's a big game tomorrow lads.

Track 3.2
Ex. It is a foul in the box.
1. It is handball on the halfway line.
2. She shoots, but it misses the goal!
3. The full back tackles the winger, and the ball goes over the touchline.

UNIT 4
Track 4.1
Jack: Harry, what's wrong?
Harry: All our equipment… all our clothes…
Jack: What happened?!
Harry: Th-They are all in the wrong place!
Jack: Oh no!
Harry: OK, OK, hold on, hold on… let's, let's, let's try and find our things.
Jack: Well, this is your shirt – number 12, right?
Harry: That's it! A-And these are your shorts… number 7, right?
Jack: Yep, they're mine. But whose black shin pads are these?
Harry: They are Miguel's!
Jack: Hmm… what about the goalkeeper gloves?
Harry: Here they are! Here are Josh's… and here are Luke's!
Jack: Great! And now… what about Tom's armband?
Harry: Good question!
Jack: Here it is! That is super important…
Harry: Not as important as my boots! Where are they?
Jack: Well, relax… nobody will steal them, they smell so bad!
Harry: Mine?! What about yours!

UNIT 5
Track 5.1
I wake up at 7:30.
I have training at 10 o'clock.
I eat lunch at 1 o'clock.
I go to bed at 11:30.

Track 5.2
Jack: Harry, look at this!
Harry: Oh wow, I love Anderson! He is a great player.
Jack: I know. It says he will move to Madrid in July, when the transfer window opens.
Harry: For like, £40 million! Amazing…
Jack: But look at this… the life of Brazilian footballers is very different.
Harry: He says he only has free time on the coach to games.
Jack: What does he do on the coach?
Harry: He says… he just… talks to friends or uses his phone.
Jack: Wow!
Harry: And here… it says he wakes up at 5am every day.
Jack: Why?
Harry: Well, in Rio de Janeiro, it's too hot to play in the afternoon, so they only train early in the morning at 7am…
Jack: No way!
Harry: Yeah, he wakes up at 5am and has training at 7am.
Jack: Then what does he do?
Harry: He has a training match at 8am.
Jack: I'm tired just listening!
Harry: Well, wait! Then he has a tactics session at 9am until 9:30, and then…
Jack: Then he can relax?
Harry: No! At 9:30am he has a skills session!
Jack: Then he can relax?!
Harry: No! He goes home at 10am, but it says he's from a poor family, so he has to do the laundry and clean his boots in the evening!
Jack: I guess he won't be doing that at Madrid!
Harry: Hahaha… I guess not!!
Jack: What else does it say?

UNIT 6
Track 6.1
1. Ow. It's my eye!
2. Come on, ref! He kicked my nose.
3. My knee hurts.
4. Ouch. He hit my eye!
5. Ref, he grabbed my neck!

Track 6.2
Jack: Pass the ball, Harry! Quick! Man on! Man on!
Harry: Ahhhhhhh!
Jack: Foul! Ref, send him off! That's a red card! I can't believe it – he has to come off…
Joe: Substitution! Miguel, you're coming on. Get ready!
Jack: Poor Harry, I hope he's OK… Harry! Harry! Are you OK?
Harry: No! Did you see that?! It was a really bad tackle!
Jack: I know! Where does it hurt?
Harry: My, my ankle… it really hurts… and my knee hurts too.
Jack: Can you walk?
Harry: I… I… I don't think so, no…

Jack:	Hold on, the physio is here!
Harry:	Thanks, Jack.
Physio:	Harry! Sit down! Are you OK? How many fingers am I holding up?
Harry:	Two! He hit my leg, not my head!

UNIT 7
Track 7.1
Jack:	How are you, Harry?
Harry:	Terrible!
Jack:	No way! Where does it hurt?
Harry:	It's my knee… it's really bad… I guess I won't be playing for a few weeks…
Jack:	No way… I'm really sorry, mate.
Harry:	Thanks, but…
Jack:	But what?
Harry:	There's more… that new player, Miguel…
Jack:	Yeah?
Harry:	What do you think of him?
Jack:	He's good… what do you think?
Harry:	He's amazing, Jack! There's no way I will get back in the team!
Jack:	Really? He is a bit short…
Harry:	So? He's really fast and very good on the ball…
Jack:	And he's left-footed?
Harry:	Oh, thanks Jack!
Jack:	Sorry…
Harry:	And what about the other new player, Luca?
Jack:	Yeah, he is really good!
Harry:	Jack!
Jack:	Sorry, again… but he's not just left-footed, he's two-footed. And tall… and strong…
Harry:	And really skilful…
Jack:	Don't worry, Harry. Everything will be OK.
Harry:	Really? Why?
Jack:	Well, the manager likes you… he thinks you're funny!
Harry:	Oh shut up, Jack!

UNIT 8
Track 8.1
1. Come on, mark up! Harry, you're on number 7.
2. Keep the ball! Stop giving it straight back to them!
3. Push up, push up! All the way to the halfway line!
4. Get tight! Don't give him any space.

Track 8.2
Jack:	Ah man, this team is really good…
Harry:	I know…
Jack:	We are lucky to only be 1 down… oh no, another corner!
Harry:	Come on, boys! Mark up! Stay close to your player!
Jack:	Luca, get tight on number 7!
Harry:	Miguel! Miguel! Get goal-side! Be strong!
Jack:	Clear it! That's it, play it long!
Harry:	Push up, push up! Don't sit back!
Jack:	Man… this is terrible.
Harry:	I know, we can't keep the ball… at all! Luca, hold the line! Get number 9 offside! Don't drop off!
Jack:	Ah, this is a disaster…
Harry:	Easy ball! Play it to feet, guys! No, Miguel, no!
Jack:	2–0… oh no…
Harry:	Disaster…
Jack:	I think your place is safe in the team.
Harry:	Wh-What do you mean?
Jack:	Well, 2–0 before half-time? The Coach is going to be very angry!

UNIT 9
Track 9.1
Joe:	Right boys, listen up.
Team:	Yes, Coach!
Joe:	Right, I'm not happy boys. I'm not happy at all. Our last match was not good. We were too slow – and our passing… terrible!
Team:	[apologizing]
Joe:	Guys, your passing was too slow, you have to move the ball quicker.
Team:	[agreeing]
Joe:	That's why we didn't score, we didn't use our pace down the channels.
Team:	[agreeing]
Joe:	And when we did attack, we were too selfish – we didn't pass the ball. Why didn't you pass, Jack?
Jack:	Sorry, erm, I-I…
Joe:	Did you see the other team? They passed the ball really well.
Team:	[agreeing]

Joe: Right! Passing drills, now! Let's go, let's go! Two-touch only! Come on boys, you can do it!
Team: [shouting encouragement]

UNIT 10
Track 10.1
Jack: So Harry, I have a question for you – who are we playing on Saturday?
Harry: Our next game? Ha! You're joking, right?! We are playing Manchester next Saturday!
Jack: Yeah, yeah, yeah. So… Manchester on Saturday. Away! What do you think?
Harry: Err… not great. They are top of the league…
Jack: And we lost our last game 2–1 to Liverpool which was…
Harry: Really bad, terrible…
Jack: But…
Harry: But… Manchester drew 1-all with Bristol.
Jack: Yeah, not a great result.
Harry: Exactly! Bristol only drew with Cardiff…
Jack: Who are bottom of the league!
Harry: And Cardiff just lost 4–1 to Newcastle!
Jack: So? Who do you think will win?
Harry: So?! I think we will win!
Jack: No doubt!
Harry: 6–0!
Jack: At least!

Answer Key

ENGLISH SPELLING AND PRONUNCIATION
Part 1: Spelling

Exercise 1
1. E
2. I
3. M
4. R
5. B
6. Q
7. W
8. A
9. V
10. Z

Exercise 2
1. Milan
2. Cairo
3. Madrid
4. Munich
5. Mexico City

Part 2: English sounds

Exercise 5
1. shoot
2. tall
3. goal
4. play
5. score
6. defender

MEET THE TEAMS
Part 1: Locomotive London Men's Team

Exercise 1
1D; 2B; 3G; 4E; 5F; 6A; 7C

Exercise 2

Club name	Locomotive London
Year founded	2017
Location	London, England
Stadium name	Champion Ground
Stadium capacity	55,000
Head Coach / age	Joe Cardoso / 43
Famous players	Luca Liberato, Taka Sato, Harry Jones

Part 2: Locomotive London Women's Team

Exercise 1
1. stadium
2. newer
3. won
4. Coach
5. captain

Exercise 2
1c; 2a; 3b

UNIT 1
Part 1: Vocabulary

Exercise 1
a. Students' own answers
b. 1B; 2A; 3D; 4C
c. full back; centre forward; central midfielder; centre back; winger; coach

Exercise 2
1. Haaland and Mbappé are forwards.
2. You're a winger.
3. Pep Guardiola is a coach.
4. Ona Batlle and Selma Bacha are full backs.
5. Bellingham is a central midfielder.
6. Students' own answers

Part 2: Grammar

Exercise 1
a. 1. **Q:** Is Mara Alber a goalkeeper?
      A: No, she isn't. She's a winger.
   2. **Q:** Are Williams and Yamal full backs?
      A: No, they aren't. They're forwards.
   3. **Q:** How old is Jude Bellingham?
      A: He's [age] years old.
   4. **Q:** Where are Maradona and Messi from?
      A: They're from Argentina.

b. Students' own answers

Part 3: Listening
Exercise 1
a. a new player
b. 1. Spain
   2. midfielder
   3. midfielder

Part 4: Practice
Exercise 1
1B; 2D; 3C; 4A; 5E; 6F

Exercise 2
Brazilian – Brazil; English – England; Spanish – Spain; Japanese – Japan; French – France; German – Germany

Exercise 3
Students' own answers

Part 5: Speaking and Writing
Exercise 1
a. 1. What is your name? My name is...
   2. How old are you? I am [age] years old.
   3. Where are you from? I am from [country name].
   4. What is your position? I am a [position name].
   5. Who is your favourite player? My favourite player is...
   6. What is your favourite thing about football? My favourite thing is...
b. Students' own answers

UNIT 2
Part 1: Vocabulary
Exercise 1
a. Students' own answers
b. 1D; 2E; 3B; 4A; 5G; 6H; 7F; 8C

Exercise 2
1. shoot
2. saves
3. head
4. passes
5. crosses
6. tackle

Part 2: Grammar
Exercise 1
1. I head
2. She fouls
3. They pass
4. they shoot

Part 3: Listening
Exercise 1
a. Students' own answers
b. Vinicius Jr, Yamal, Wirtz, Haaland
c. Wirtz: Passes ✓; Scores ✗
   Williams: Tackles ✓; Crosses ✓
   Yamal: Tackles ✗; Heads ✗; Scores ✓
   Haaland: Heads ✓; Scores ✓

Part 4: Practice
Exercise 1
1. don't
2. don't
3. don't
4. doesn't
5. don't _____

Part 5: Speaking and Writing
Exercise 1
a. 1. What's your name? My name is [name].
   2. How old are you? I'm [age] years old.
   3. Where are you from? I'm from [country name].
   4. What's your position? I'm a(n) [position name].
   5. On your team, who shoots the most? [Name] shoots the most!
   6. On your team, who tackles the most? [Name] tackles the most!
   7. On your team, who passes the most? [Name] passes the most!
   8. On your team, who saves the most? [Name] saves the most!
b. Students' own answers

UNIT 3
Part 1: Vocabulary

Exercise 1
1C; 2B; 3F; 4A; 5D; 6E

Exercise 2
1D; 2A; 3E; 4B; 5C; 6F

Exercise 3
a. 1. on the touchline
2. in the box
3. in the centre circle
4. the corner flag

b. Students' own answers

Part 2: Listening

Exercise 1
a. penalty, free kick, corner
b. Jack (J): takes corners (left); takes free kicks (right); takes penalties
Harry (H): takes corners (right); takes free kicks (left)
c. Students' own answers

Exercise 2
1. free kick
2. goal kick
3. throw-in

Part 3: Grammar

Exercise 1
1. Jack doesn't take penalties.
2. Harry and Jack take free kicks
3. Who takes free kicks from the left?
4. Goalkeepers don't take corners.
5. Do you take throw-ins?
6. Students' own answers

Part 4: Practice

Exercise 1
1. It's a throw-in. – B
2. It's a free kick. – D
3. It's a foul. – A
4. It's offside. – E
5. It's handball. – C

Exercise 2
Scene B: The winger crosses the ball, then the defender handballs it, so it's a penalty.
Scene C: He takes a corner and the striker heads it. He scores (a goal)!

Part 5: Speaking and Writing

Exercise 1
1. takes
2. Do
3. Does
4. do
5. does

Part 6: Extra time

Exercise 1
1. touchline
2. box
3. take
4. spot
5. scores

Exercise 2
Students' own answers

UNIT 4
Part 1: Vocabulary

Exercise 1
a. Boots; Shirt; Shorts; Socks
b. 1. Their shorts are blue. – B
2. His socks are black. – F
3. His shirt is white. – C
4. Your shin pads are green. – D
5. Her gloves are yellow. – E
6. My boots are orange. – A

Exercise 2
who = whose; I = my; you = your; he = his; she = her; they = their; we = our; Lucy = Lucy's

Part 2: Listening

Exercise 1
a. their football kit

b.

Kit	Name
Shirt number 12	Harry
Shorts number 7	Jack
Black shin pads	Miguel
Goalkeeper gloves	Josh and Luke
Armband	Tom

Part 3: Grammar
Exercise 1
1. This is my shirt.
2. ✓
3. Whose socks are these?
4. These are my shin pads.
5. ✓

Part 4: Practice
Exercise 1
a. 1. **Q:** Are these socks Liam's?
   A: No, they aren't his. They're Luca's.
2. **Q:** Is this shirt Luca's?
   A: Yes, it's his.
3. **Q:** Whose gloves are these?
   A: They're Sarah's.
4. **Q:** Are these shorts yours?
   A: No, they aren't (mine).

b. me = my = mine; you = your = yours; he = his = his; she = her = hers; they = their = theirs

Part 5: Review
Exercise 1
a. Florian Wirtz <u>are</u> a football player. <u>He from</u> Germany. He <u>are</u> a central midfielder. He <u>plays</u> corners and penalties. This is <u>her</u> shirt! Germany wear a white shirt, black shorts and <u>orange</u> socks.

b. Students' own answers

UNIT 5
Part 1: Vocabulary
Exercise 1
a. Students' own answers
b. 1. have training
   2. have breakfast / eat lunch / have dinner
   3. wake up
   4. use my phone / check social media
   5. go home / use my phone
   6. go to bed / sleep
c. 1C; 2A; 3B; 4F
d. 1. I wake up at 7:30.
   2. I have training at 10 o'clock.
   3. I eat lunch at 1 o'clock.
   4. I go to bed at 11:30.
e. 1. have breakfast
   2. have training
   3. have a match
   4. have free time
   5. go to the gym
   6. go to bed
   7. go shopping
   8. go home
f. Students' own answers

Part 2: Listening
Exercise 1
i. Brazil

Exercise 2
a.

Anderson's daily schedule	
Time	Activity
5am	wake up
7am	training
8am	training match
9am	tactics session
9:30am	skills session
10am	go home

b. Students' own answers

Part 3: Grammar
Exercise 1
1. I eat/have dinner at 9pm.
2. She eats/has breakfast at the training ground.
3. They go to bed at midnight!
4. He goes to training in the morning.
5. My team don't go to the shopping mall at the weekend.
6. When do you eat/have lunch?
7. What time does your best friend go home?

Part 4: Practice
Exercise 1
Students' own answers

Exercise 2
1. is
2. am
3. have
4. In
5. at
6. eat/have
7. do
8. go
9. eat/have
10. don't
11. do

Exercise 3
a. 1b; 2a; 3c
b. Students' own answers

UNITS 1–5 REVIEW
Exercise 1
1. They are defenders. – B
2. He is a goalkeeper. – A
3. She is a forward. – E
4. I am a central midfielder. – C
5. You are a winger. – D

Exercise 2
1. Eduardo <u>takes</u> penalties for our team.
2. Ji So-Yun's boots <u>are</u> red.
3. Holland play in orange <u>shirts</u>.
4. Jamal Musiala <u>doesn't</u> take corners.
5. <u>Her</u> shorts are blue.
6. Mia <u>is</u> from Canada.

Exercise 3
1d; 2c; 3b; 4e; 5a

UNIT 6
Part 1: Vocabulary
Exercise 1
a. 1. back
    2. leg
    3. chest
    4. shoulder
    5. arm
b. hair; ear; eye; nose; mouth; neck
c. 2. nose
    3. knee
    4. eye
    5. neck

Exercise 2
a. Students' own answers
b. 1. ankle
    2. thigh
    3. hamstring
    4. knee
    5. shin

Exercise 3
Students' own answers

Part 2: Listening
Exercise 1
a. i.
b. 1B; 2A; 3C; 4D

Part 3: Grammar
Exercise 1
a. 1. i.
    2. ii.
    3. ii.
    4. can't
b. 1. Can forwards use their hands? No, they can't.
    2. Can midfielders pass? Yes, they can.
    3. Can referees tackle? No, they can't.
    4. Does Rodrygo play for Mexico? No, he doesn't.
    5. Can you play in midfield? Yes, I can./No, I can't.

Answer Key

Part 4: Practice

Exercise 1
1. **A:** Where does it hurt?
   B: My eye.
2. **A:** Are you OK?
   B: No, it's my ankle.
   A: Can you carry on?
   B: No, I can't. I think I have to come off.
3. **A:** Where does it hurt?
   B: My nose.
   A: Does this hurt?
   B: Ouch! Yes, it does.

Exercise 2
Jack: Harry! Man <u>on</u>!
Harry: Ouch! My leg!
Physio: <u>Are</u> you OK, Harry?
Harry: No, my knee <u>hurts</u>!
Physio: <u>Does</u> this hurt?
Harry: Yes! Yes!
Physio: OK, you have to come <u>off</u>!

UNIT 7
Part 1: Vocabulary

Exercise 1
slow ← → fast
overweight ← → slim
tall ← → short
small ← → big
weak ← → strong

Exercise 2
1. He is a fast winger.
2. She is a strong defender.
3. They are tall midfielders.
4. He is a short and weak goalkeeper.
5. He is a weak forward.

Exercise 3
a. 1A; 2E; 3C/D; 4C/D; 5B
b. Students' own answers

Part 2: Listening

Exercise 1
a. i.

b.

Miguel	Luca
Short ✓	Fast
Fast ✓	Two-footed ✓
Strong	Tall ✓
Good on the ball ✓	Strong ✓
Left-footed ✓	Skilful ✓

c. Students' own answers

Part 3: Grammar

Exercise 1
1. is
2. tall
3. not
4. Are
5. forward

Exercise 2
1. He<u>'s</u> a very fast winger.
2. They're very <u>strong</u> defenders.
3. She's <u>a weak</u> goalkeeper.
4. My teammates <u>are</u> so good at football!

What a goal!
wide, B; over, G; the post, C; the crossbar, H; roof of the net, F; top corner, A/I; bottom right, J; top right, I; bottom corner D/J; the middle, E

1: Yes, great goal!; What a goal!; Great strike!

2: Oh, it hit the woodwork!; Great save!; Oh, unlucky!; It was off-target!; Oh, just wide!

Part 4: Practice

Exercise 1
1B; 2C; 3D; 4A

Exercise 2
Students' own answers

UNIT 8
Part 1: Vocabulary

Exercise 1
a. 1A; 2B; 3C; 4D; 5E; 6F; 7H; 8G; 9I; 10J; 11K; 12L
b. Students' own answers

Exercise 2
2. Keep the ball!
3. Push up!
4. Get tight!

Exercise 3
1d; 2c; 3a; 4b

Part 2: Listening

Exercise 1
a. ii.
b. A. Get tight! – 2
   B. Don't drop off! – 8
   C. Play it long! – 4
   D. Mark up! – 1
   E. Clear it! – 3
   F. Push up! – 5
   G. Hold the line! – 7
   H. Keep the ball! – 6
c. 1J; 2I; 3I

Exercise 2
Students' own answers

Part 3: Grammar

Exercise 1
1. goal
2. Don't
3. it
4. it
5. on

Exercise 2
1. Mark <u>up</u>!
2. <u>Man</u> on!
3. Clear <u>it</u>!
4. Switch <u>it</u>!
5. Easy <u>ball</u>!
6. <u>Hold</u> the line!

Ball game
A: 1, 2, 4, 5; B: 3; C: 6

Part 4: Practice

Exercise 1
2. Switch it!
3. Hold the line!
4. Play it long!

Exercise 2
1. is
2. on
3. well
4. isn't
5. mark
6. hold
7. onside
8. off

Exercise 3
a. Students' own answers
b. Students' own answers

UNIT 9
Part 1: Vocabulary

Exercise 1
Students' own answers

Exercise 2
a. 1D; 2C; 3B; 4A
b. 1B; 2A; 3C; 4D
c. Students' own answers

Exercise 3
shoot

Exercise 4
/d/ = scored, squared, dribbled
/t/ = passed, switched, pressed
/ɪd/ = headed, created

The foot
1. Stop the ball
2. Goal kick, Dribble
3. Cross
4. Cross
5. –

Part 2: Listening

Exercise 1
a. ii.
b. 1. were
2. was
3. score
4. didn't
5. passed
c. Students' own answers

Part 3: Grammar

Exercise 1
1. She was so strong.
2. They were quite slow on the counterattack.
3. He wasn't a top goal-scorer.
4. She was an international defender.

Exercise 2
1. scored
2. cleared
3. was
4. didn't
5. were
6. Did
7. tackled

Exercise 3
1. He <u>was</u> a great player!
2. He <u>didn't</u> square the ball!
3. She didn't <u>pass</u> the ball!
4. It <u>was</u> a brilliant game, just brilliant!
5. They <u>were</u> a terrible team!

Part 4: Practice

Exercise 1
1. The winger dribbled the ball forward, but the full back fouled him. Then the midfielder took the free kick.
2. The centre back squared the ball, then the full back dribbled towards the box and passed it to the forward. The forward shot at goal.
3. The defender played it long to the winger. He created a chance for the forward who scored a goal.

Let's play!
1C; 2A; 3B

Exercise 2
1. played
2. was
3. scored
4. was
5. penalty
6. crossed
7. were
8. missed

UNIT 10
Part 1: Vocabulary

1. i.
2. iii.
3. i.
4. i.

Grammar note
win – won; draw – drew; lose – lost

Exercise 2
1. Corinthians beat São Paulo two–one.
2. Real Madrid and Barcelona drew three-all.
3. Fenerbahçe beat Galatasary one–nil.
4. Juventus lost two–one.

Exercise 3
Students' own answers

Exercise 4
1. Manchester Athletic are top of the league with 67 points.
2. Liverpool City are second.
3. Locomotive London have 63 points. They're third.
4. Cardiff Central are bottom of the league.
5. Newcastle Town are in sixth.
6. Bristol FC are fourth in the league.

Exercise 5
Students' own answers

Part 2: Listening

Exercise 1
a. 1. ii.
2. i.
b. Locomotive London 1–2 Liverpool City
Bristol FC 1–1 Manchester Athletic
Newcastle Town 4–1 Cardiff Central

Exercise 2
Students' own answers

Part 3: Grammar
Exercise 1
1. We're playing Liverpool next Sunday. – F
2. I think Manchester will win. – P
3. Bristol are playing Newcastle tomorrow. – F
4. I think Cardiff will lose. – P
5. Birmingham are playing against Manchester on Wednesday. – F

Exercise 2
2. We're playing <u>at</u> home tomorrow.
3. I think Real Madrid <u>will</u> draw next week.
4. Tottenham are <u>playing</u> Arsenal on Saturday!
5. I think the game will be <u>0–0</u>.

Part 4: Practice
Exercise 1
Students' own answers

Exercise 2
1. They're
2. on
3. will
4. beat
5. won
6. home
7. thinks
8. away
9. lose

REVIEW UNITS 6–10
Exercise 1
1c; 2e; 3a; 4d; 5b

Exercise 2
1. Real Madrid <u>won</u> last week against Manchester United.
2. Messi <u>was</u> incredible yesterday – two goals and an assist, amazing!
3. What <u>did you do</u> last week? Did you train a lot?
4. I was surprised Chelsea didn't <u>lose</u> the final.
5. When <u>was</u> our tactics session, did I miss it?

Exercise 3
1. top
2. think
3. away
4. drew
5. will

Notes

Also available from HATRIQA®

Football English Elementary Workbook

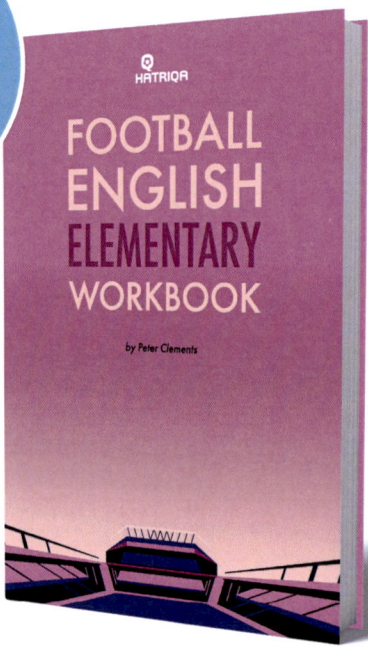

Learn to speak English like a Premier League Star

The workbook is a companion for the textbook. It is a self-study book allowing learners to work at their own pace and review and consolidate the content from the book. Each unit mirrors the same unit from the textbook, making it easy to navigate, and contains answers in the back of the book.

Available now at
www.hatriqa.com

Language Learner Notebooks

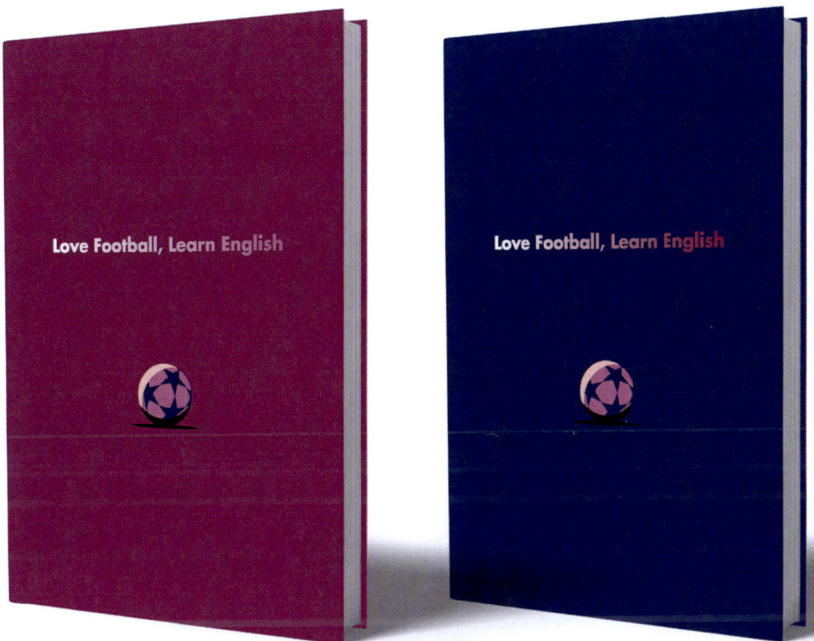

HATRIQA Language Learner Notebooks are football-themed vocabulary notebooks for English. They are easy to use and are the perfect complement to HATRIQA's other materials to help you remember language more quickly.

Available now at
www.hatriqa.com

Jamie Johnson Graded Readers

"I almost feel like I am Jamie Johnson now!"
JUDE BELLINGHAM

Based on the novels by Dan Freedman, the Jamie Johnson series tells the story of a boy who lives and breathes soccer. He has great skills, and he wants to get to the top. In each book in the series, we see Jamie as he learns more and follows his dream. He plans to become one of the greatest soccer players in the world.

HATRIQA's Soccer Reader® Series comprises the best in soccer fiction written as graded books for learners of English as a foreign language.

Available in paperback and ebook at
www.hatriqa.com

Printed and bound by CPI Group (UK) Ltd, Croydon, CR0 4YY
03/10/2025
01968512-0002